THE JOY
STRATEGIST

YOUR
PATH TO
INNER
CHANGE

GRACE
HARRY

&
ANDSCAPE
LOS ANGELES   NEW YORK

All rights reserved. Published by Andscape Books, an imprint
of Buena Vista Books, Inc. No part of this book may be reproduced
or transmitted in any form or by any means, electronic or mechanical,
including photocopying, recording, or by any information storage
and retrieval system, without written permission from the publisher.
For information address Andscape Books, 77 West 66th Street,
New York, New York 10023.

First Edition, October 2023

10 9 8 7 6 5 4 3 2 1

FAC-058958-23236

Printed in the United States of America

This book is set in Avenir, Avenir Next, Abril, and Helvetica Neue

Designed by Amy C. King

Library of Congress Cataloging-in-Publication Number: 2023931772

ISBN 978-1-368-09264-7

Reinforced binding

www.AndscapeBooks.com

THIS BOOK IS A DEDICATION
TO THE BREAKING OPEN OF MY HEART
IN MANY DIFFERENT DIRECTIONS.

How to InJOY This Book

When I took the very first steps on my JOY journey, resources were tight. I was a newly separated, single mother of two. The only support I could afford was going to local meetings of various 12-step programs. Through the help of those programs, as well as other free resources, I began to see my pain as a gift—the complications that happened to me paved a pathway for learning how to live in JOY.

This has been my life's greatest education: how to live in JOY, even amid struggles, challenges, and turmoil. And that's why I wrote this book. Like me back then, you may not be able to see the open door right now. You may hardly see a bright day ahead, let alone a life lived with JOY. I know, because I've been there, too. And it's why I'm getting naked in this book. I'm going to tell you my un-touched-up stories, my unvarnished truth, and my unbelievably painful experiences—all with the hope that the lessons contained within can help you rediscover your JOY.

Over time, and with a lot of work, I found a way to push through. But it wasn't a straight line. There was no simple checklist, no five-point program. Hence the structure of this book, which is presented as more of a lyrical essay than a user's manual. I want you to lean into the feeling of ease and flow that naturally arises as we lean into THE WORK. The book is packed with tips, tools, and exercises to help you cultivate your JOY, embrace a more fulfilling life, and overcome obstacles.

This book is also a physical experience as much as it is a literary one. For example, whenever you see ◄━━━━ I want you to take a full breath, from your seat to your crown. Fully expand into each place in your body, allowing the breath to travel; allow it to fill you like a balloon. From your heart, feeling into the ideas, questions, and connections before moving on to the next paragraph or page.

Why? Because I also didn't learn until later in life that JOY is deeply tied to what's happening in our bodies. And for me, one of the most powerful ways I've cultivated JOY is through physical movement, breathing exercises, and appreciating that the mind and body have a distinct connection.

I am honest and vulnerable throughout the book to encourage you to be honest and vulnerable as well. These are the building blocks to discovering your JOY, and you need both honesty and vulnerability to explore your emotions, thoughts, and behaviors. Your brain may resist at first, but if you lean into your heart and what it is trying to share, you will be supported the whole way.

You'll also notice that I share lessons I've learned from many different sources, without naming them. The reason being that when we create our early survivor character, we safeguard it with a ton of security measures to keep it in line: *I like this, I don't like that, I agree with that human and not that one.* A list of personal Dos and Don'ts. I don't want to shove my teachers down your throat. We all have to create our own toolbox of what will help us guide ourselves back to JOY, every second.

The Joy Strategist is designed to be interactive and practical. I encourage you to set aside time to read and reflect on parts that speak to you. Take your time to fully digest each concept before moving on to the next. This isn't homework. There's no exam. I'm not going to emerge in your dreams and ask if you read every last word on page 88. This book is an invitation, and it's about you—your time, your space, your JOY. You can read the book straight through, or you can dip in and out as life requires. The choice is yours.

Along the way, embrace both the low peaks and high valleys—and understand how they help us at each step. Here we go.

Let the revolution of JOY . . . begin!

Intro

*If your HEART was
an animated cartoon,
what would it look like
and what would be
its theme song?*

The Evolution Begins

started to feel light-headed and queasy. That was a rare feeling for me in my body in those days. I always felt physically pretty good—strong and energetic, no matter what I was going through. I was attending an event in Colorado, and someone suggested I go into an oxygen bar, a chill space where you can get hooked up to an oxygen tank to alleviate altitude sickness, which is what I was suffering from. I was with an eclectic crew of artists, agents, and managers who decided to come with me. As we walked into the oxygen bar, we felt the proverbial purse clutch, the uncomfortableness of the others there. That was such a foreign feeling for me at the time, but I don't know if I allowed those feelings in in the past. I was always so excited, interested by whatever I was about to encounter.

My crew, sadly used to this greeting, experienced the natural reaction one has to knee-jerk prejudice, and immediately felt defensive. One wanted to leave. One wanted to over-prove. One wanted to fix. I felt the need to share, so I positioned myself in the one chair that was closest to the Others, while everyone else moved as far away from them as possible.

The open-hearted way I introduced myself encouraged one person to try to connect with me. Needing to somehow justify themself, they proceeded to tell me a story. They said they were recently flying first class when some others (another eclectic and diverse group of artists) they hadn't expected to encounter in the same privileged space they were inhabiting appeared.

They felt threatened by the artists in that moment, but more to the point, they voiced that they blamed them for negatively influencing their child with their dress, sound, and energy.

They were deeply uncomfortable with the power of the artists' collective voice, style, and the culture at large. Despite finding the story to be sad, offensive, and ignorant, I persevered in my conversation. I discerned that they were not someone who knew how to or wanted to connect or be in right relation with all the others who inhabit this beautiful earth school. Rapid spiritual evolution is possible for all souls. As uncomfortable and challenging as human life can be on this planet, it is a wonderful place for our growth, experimentation, and evolution.

I believe we have each been deployed to carry out this mission of personal transformation: allowing Earth to provide us with incredible opportunities for learning and expansion. For that reason, and to tie into the concept of beginner's mind, that is why I call it EARTH SCHOOL.

I then asked what their perception of me was. They launched right into "Oh, well . . . you . . ." (This was something I'd heard many times before.)

"You instantly made me and everyone here feel comfortable. . . . We can relate to you. . . . You share a similar upbringing, a similar education, and you're clearly comfortable in our social circles. . . ." Humans are constantly striving for comfort, certainty, and safety, not necessarily growth, and that fact was laid out for me right there.

I asked, "Can I tell you a story?"

I shared about a human with a complicated mixture of realities, multiple lineages that don't necessarily play well together. A human who came into earth school with a heavy backpack containing the epigenetic stories, traumas, and triumphs of their mixed bag of ancestors. At birth they were put into foster care, and when their very young birth mother finally got them back, they were uprooted and moved around a lot throughout their childhood. Their mother, choosing to have them against a lot of odds, advice, and little support from their core family, had very few resources. I then asked them what their thoughts were about that human I mentioned in my story. They went into all these weird stories and judgments. "Well, that human's probably a . . ." Blah, blah, blah, blah, blah, blah—all negative.

I took a breath and kept my heart open. I revealed that the story is my story (more of which I will tell in later chapters) and saw them slowly begin to awaken to the idea that their knee-jerk assumptions, their purse-clutching, their programmed fears, had no relationship to reality. By the end of the conversation, I felt proud, because without attacking or torture-porning or story one-upping, I planted some beautiful seeds that they could take into their communities and spread through JOY.

A new tool to replace fear.

Ahhhhh, the feeling of impacting the human experience through Love, sharing, connecting, and JOY. I made a commitment to myself to move closer to the people and situations that scared me the most, and to use those interactions and experiences as remedies to share for healing, growth, and evolution in consciousness. I am not naive enough to think that this is an easy solution or even one that is appropriate for all people in all circumstances. I don't mean to be coy. I did not use the words *racism* or *classism* on purpose. I do not mean to diminish the power and potency of those words or systems of oppression, but I do mean to demonstrate the empowering truth that we are the ones who choose how we react to situations and OUR world.

In that moment, I gave myself permission to view myself in a new way. I gave myself permission to envision myself in the way I wanted to be. I dared to imagine a world I would like to live in. I let go of the FICTION of LIMITATION. Everything starts in the imagination. When we feel the Other has changed, it's just that we have actually gotten to know ourselves and them more intimately and in TRUTH.

HEART is the full-body **YES**. The "you'll see!" because it's so clear to me. Comfort, imagination, spontaneity, **FUN**! An embodied deep, sensual knowing of all there is. The great lover of your emotional energy, the wise sage guiding your feelings. An internal confidence of light and promise. The magic GPS in all of us, when turned on. When you really listen to your heart, it's teaching you a different way of knowing.

Beginner's Mind

Obviously, JOY is not a four-letter word. And yet, for most of my life it's felt like one. In my story, JOY was a word so corny you wouldn't catch me saying it out loud. A word for greeting cards and fussy old people on TV. But now I say it all the time. JOY, JOY, JOY! The now me is proud to identify as one of the most JOYful people I know.

What IS delicious to say out loud is that after decades working with some of the entertainment industry's biggest artists globally, I've given it all up in the name of JOY. Why? Because JOY is the most important experience we can have, and we must make time for JOY every single day. It's that important— up there with food, sleep, or air.

I had to land unjoyfully inside another divorce to finally figure that out. There I was at the end of my marriage, back in the same situation with the same emotions, and the same sad sense of the universe doing me wrong . . . again. They say the third time's the charm. It finally got me to wake up by revealing to me how I played a huge hand in all of it. Jumping off the ride wouldn't mean much without stopping to ask the really big questions:

What did I want?

What was I going to have to change to get it?

What was I going to DO about it?

Thinking about what I wanted? Ouch. I'd never really exercised that muscle before—the one that has the strength to push past all the bizarre societal beliefs of what we should and shouldn't do. The one that understands that you don't have to be married, successful, ready for sex all the time, cook five-course meals, entertain the community, love every in-law, and procreate. The one that is strong enough to lift what you truly want from deep in your gut and hold it up in broad daylight for you yourself to see.

What did I want?

Most of us don't know shit about feeling joyful. Most of us take the feeling when it comes in a passive, obedient way. We wait like good little children for the universe to bestow "IT" upon us. But JOY is not an afterthought; it's not the loot bag you get at the end of the party. JOY is the main event, the most important thing that can happen to you every day. It's responsible for your understanding of what you want out of this life and for guiding the decisions you make on the way to getting it. JOY determines who you welcome into your life, who you trust, and who | how you love.

As kids, we live in our feelings, and we expect to feel JOY. We even feel entitled to it. By the time we're adults, JOY becomes elusive. The instinct gets buried under pressure from our parents, our friends, society, everyone. We become people pleasers and self-saboteurs. Think about it. When you were a kid, you didn't have to go looking for JOY. You would stand next to a pole and start twirling around it or kicking your leg or singing a song for no reason.

When did you lose that?

And where did it go?

As a society, we've gotten far away from our own truth. We're being held captive inside man-made constructs that are not real. We're sold propaganda that love outside of ourselves heals us. "You complete me." Yes, love changes you, but we are not taught first how to be in relationship with the love inside our own hearts. I am an advocate for systemic inner change, which is what comes before effective and authentic systemic outer change.

JOY is the Paradigm Shift.

What Is a Beginner's Mind?

Having a beginner's mind means you approach the world through beginner's eyes. The term is translated from the original word, *shoshin*, which is a word that comes from Zen Buddhism. It refers to having an attitude of openness, eagerness, and lack of preconceptions. You look at every situation you're placed in as if it's the first time you are seeing it. When studying a subject, even when studying at an advanced level, you approach it just as a beginner would.

If we employ the "beginner's mind," we can drop our number-one saboteur, or the expectations and preconceived, socially constructed ideas that were instilled by society, and see instead with our child eyes just like a beginner. If you've ever learned something new, you can remember what that's like. You were probably confused, because you didn't know how to do whatever you were learning, but you were also looking at everything as if it was brand-new, perhaps with curiosity and wonder. That's beginner's mind. This concept—now my mission—was new to me five years ago. I had to rebirth my childhood so that I could chip off all the fear that was cemented around my heart.

Making the decision to do what is right for your life is not easy; it takes courage and strength to step out of something that's not working, look at it honestly, own your piece of it, and decide to make a change. That kind of ripple in your life creates a huge wave for all involved. Stand tall in knowing that you are taking the first step to reclaim your life and set the course for its inevitable growth. By releasing your past—in this lifetime, as well as your ancestral DNA—and honoring what you learned from it, you can create space for all the magic that a brand-new start offers.

JOY is Our Birthright.

First things first: JOY IS one of our most basic needs. Before you work for anyone else, every single day of your life, you need to tap into your own JOY. Only then will you begin to make choices that support it. Tap into your JOY and you'll learn to choose yourself first. Do one thing every day that brings you JOY.

That's what I want you to do. Literally. That's an order.

JOY is not a luxury.

It's your birthright.

STEP ONE ON YOUR PATH TO JOY is to assemble a toolbox of techniques and activities that spark JOY for you. This might, at first, be harder than you think.

If you ask a friend what brings them JOY, don't be surprised when they get too tongue-tied to answer. We all take for granted that we know what brings us JOY, but most of us lose track of it. I know that I was only able to get my head around the idea of JOY when I thought back to my eleven-year-old self.

I felt happiest and most free when I was eleven. And one of the things I loved most at eleven was getting on a swing. Remember being eleven? That was the last time I really felt I was living for myself—before hormones started raging and I got hung up on being alluring for other people. Don't get me wrong, even at eleven things weren't easy. But every time I'd get on a swing and go high above the ground, I felt like everything would be okay. I felt lighter and connected to a bigger something.

As an adult, looking for my lost JOY, one of the first things I learned was the value of reincorporating play into my life. It's so valuable, I swear I'll do anything for the JOY that playfulness brings. I'll break out the Hula-Hoop, jump on a trampoline, make a playlist of songs that transport me to all the best moments of being me. Coloring, changing the lights' colors for a sexy dance party. I'll write. I'll go somewhere to sit on a swing. I'll get dressed up and wear costumes outside. I'll make up songs. If I only have a bit of time, I'll read something short that makes me laugh. There's no excuse not to play a little every day—even if it's just for a minute.

The thing about JOY is that it gets you closer to understanding what it is you want. It begins to rearrange your life, making you the star of your own story. Not only does that JOY seep into other things you do, the act of taking the time to experience JOY is really important. When you make time for JOY—when you give yourself permission to play—it is the ultimate act of self-care. If you're playing, you're not doing it for anyone else. Your enjoyment is the only priority—and you just can't be worrying about who you want to please and everything you should and shouldn't be doing when you're playing. In those moments when you let yourself matter most, you're bound to discover more about your personal truth.

Building the Toolbox of JOY

F eeling your way out of the dark requires a toolbox of support—practices that connect instantly to your heart. It's a choice to start each new day committed to living JOYfully, to making JOY your North Star. The tools I use might not work for you, so I recommend that you start by exploring your Self. Look through old photos and journals, ask your family what they remember about you when you were younger. Allow yourself to daydream, to connect with your body, mind, and heart. To begin to pull up and remember the moments when you experienced deep JOY in your life.

We are all taught daily rituals for feeding ourselves and getting dressed but rarely are we taught how to start every day in a state of JOY. After much searching and seeking, I have finally found the right combination of joyful pursuits that now make up my daily feel-incredible-all-day ritual. I practice some combination of yoga, dance, free writing, meditation, chanting, prayers, Reiki precepts, Orisha songs, and free (aimless, from the heart, not for transaction) play.

However, when I first made the decision to approach life through the energy of JOY, I tried everything, and I mean everything, in my pursuit of JOY-filled experiences. I suspect my friends were beginning to worry about me, as my skin shedding was complicated, even to watch. As I opened my child eyes and heart and connected with my beginner's mind, interesting invitations and opportunities began coming in—a silent retreat, Burning Man, breath work in the jungle, a Hoffman Institute workshop, spa trips, job offers, even a young lover!

In the 12-Step Program, there is an expression. "Your old life [aka behavior] does not want to go in to memory." Meaning that we kept ourselves safe inside a persona (the helpful one, the sweet one) and that when we begin to let our hearts lead, it changes our behavior. Brain and ego work hard to remind us how scary and uncertain that could be. Trying to frighten us back in to submission. I find that true for old relationship dynamics, too.

But it wasn't until I attended a three-day healing event that I felt the beginning of my unfolding. The organizer, a profoundly brilliant human, shared about their ceremonies and how the icebreaker and entrance is writing your own obituary | eulogy. I first approached the task like I did all things then, with a ferocity that misses all the jewels. It was, as I should have imagined, challenging. When completed, the truth that my own soul revealed to me was magic.

My Eulogy

Celebrating the life of Grace,
aka Apple Head.

She was the daughter,
granddaughter, wife,
mother of _____.

Born in Staten Island,
raised in Brooklyn,
a wildcat of a human.
Deliciously curious,
constantly joyful,
full of passion and life.
Lived her life in dedication to service,
the first fifty to all. Transcended to
live the second half in service as the
embodiment of JOY.

And the Award Goes To . . .

I f writing your obituary feels too intimidating, then you can pick it up from a different handle. I also learned a lot from watching many of my loves win awards, all of which required writing an acceptance speech (really a kind of eulogy) that made them reflect back on their life and what they accomplished, the kind of person they are | were, what they did for others, and the lessons of it all. In many ways it's what gives our lives meaning—the fact that we're mortal.

When we reflect back on our lives, who we are, what we value, and perhaps what we regret become crystal clear.

My Acceptance Speech

I first have to thank . . .

LOVE.

I didn't get it. Wow. You were right. Thank you for your patience with me, which I now know IS love.

Searching for you for a lifetime, not understanding that I had a plethora. My mother, father, grandparents, sisters, friends, lovers, personal and professional partners, children, teachers, mentors, fellow illuminators, in the way they understood love. And then Love again, for teaching me that all is fueled by my love of ME. In the sweetest, most subtle way, the profound way, in the hug-and-slap way, and in the *It's-not-about-me* way.

Multiple decades proving my worth and value to others, looking for praise through self-sacrifice. It is staggering to think about what I could have accomplished early in my life if I applied that same energy, focus, and commitment to myself. And then the last five amazing years. All of it leading me to today.

From my full heart.

This first exercise will be the one to shape the list of tools YOU will need to build YOUR toolbox.

TO KICK THINGS OFF

Take three cleansing deep breaths and
three releasing exhalations.

BREATHE IN FOR FOUR COUNTS. . . .

HOLD FOR SEVEN. . . .

BREATHE OUT FOR EIGHT. . . .

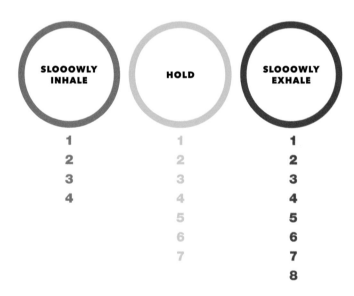

DO THIS THREE TIMES,

and smile when you are finished.

It's time for your JOY Revolution. . . . Are you ready?

Now

Go ahead and write your eulogy or your acceptance speech!

You're welcome!

The processes and exercises in this book will take the exact amount of time you offer them. It's entirely up to you. The point isn't to follow my process to the letter, but instead to adopt the steps and then adapt them to what feels right for you. The one thing I ask: Handwrite the lists that correspond to the exercises throughout the book. I do most of my writing on my computer because my handwriting is hard to read. But for this book's rituals, it is important to handwrite, as the act of writing by hand unleashes creativity and increases neural activity in certain sections of the brain, much like meditation.

I

*We miss the high valleys,
running through them to
get to another low peak.*

Everything IS Everything

The way you do one thing
is the way you do everything.
The way you feel anything
is the way you feel everything.

We try to compartmentalize our lives, separate oneself from another self—but that's not the way it works. That need to compartmentalize has led us to become disconnected from our bodies, our ecosystems, our hearts, and ultimately our essence. You only begin to live luminously when you figure out what works in one area—and then take that same show on the road for every other part of your life.

That can be a gift, if what you have learned up to this point has taught you what does work for YOU.

I, on the other hand, manafucked myself for years by running the script in my head that I'm a high school dropout. Thus, uneducated, not smart enough, and therefore not entitled to _____. I led from the place of striving beyond what I truly had skills for, could really do, hiding the fact that I believed myself a fraud and had to achieve higher and do more to actually be what I said I was. I figured it out every time, until I had an *Oh no* moment. When I surrender to their magic and new directions, those giant detours always introduce me to parts of my higher-vibrating self.

I began to understand that each scenario was just a lesson, a reminder that I can survive.

Over and over again.

When the game is played InJOY, you actually Thrive.

This deep understanding opened things up into a wider, more beautiful lens of that belief and is the foundation of everything I do.

I worked with an incredible life coach who pointed out to me that the way I parent my children and bestow love to all I fall in love with is my life's curriculum. That I already had THE PLAN, the method to be used in every other area of my life. Eureka!!!

I can achieve anything else in my life in every area if I approach it with unapologetic beginner's mind.

Like parenting. I got it because I came into the role with so little concept of what it entailed that going in with a beginner's mind came naturally. Funny that we need so much accreditation to "achieve" so much on earth school, YET every new parent can only apply for the job with absolutely no experience or true preparation. Only amateurs can be first-time parents. And since I had the gift of a blank slate of the "rules" of parenting, I approached it like it was my life's guru. I wanted them to have the childhood I wanted for myself, and at the same time, I somehow understood that my real role as a caregiver was to get out of their way. Loaded with a giant bag of life tools for when they graduated from my school and moved on to life's giant university.

I come from a long line of humans who for the most part had to parent themselves. And not because their basic needs were neglected, but because who they felt they were was different than everyone else around them, and for the survival and growth of the species, they had to create a new way. Pioneers of a sort. So, when I got pregnant I had as my main tool that my parents taught me *At the very least, I can figure it out.* Then life taught me listening to myself, which I later learned is my own GPS.

I can do this, so how do I do everything else? I think about the end goal and then create the steps backward to today's first small step. Boot-Camping Future Adults. They pointed out to me that same concept, structure, and methodology IS *everything is everything.* My own on-the-job training of life.

In this era of extreme polarization or radical separation, the issues that are bubbling up right now—race, sexual preference, gender identity, income inequality, etc.—signify a profound shift in our world that is about evolving out of separation into higher levels of consciousness and thus connection. Consciousness is the power of Light, an energy and a quality that does not force or exploit, but honors free will and the presence of all people.

YOU . . . are the World!

Living in the Light is to be living in a state of . . .

MAHABA

Arabic word for living in a state of LOVE.

NAMASTE

A word derived from Sanskrit, meaning
I bow to you, or
The divine in me sees the divine in you.

FURAHA

Swahili word for feelings of JOY and happiness when used to encourage someone else.

XIAN

The Chinese word *xian* is translatable into English as (in Daoist philosophy and cosmology) *spiritually immortal; transcendent human; celestial being.*

VIVERE ALLA LUCE

Italian for living in the light.

It is a simple acknowledgment of our Oneness.

Getting hooked into who did what to whom can drive people to insanity. Although you may feel passionately about certain issues in the outside world, in the end, things don't shift until we shift ourselves by drawing from the Light and bringing consciousness within.

Being a Light holder means that there is a certain integrity to holding the Light and choosing to let go of all the outside stuff. We cannot change outer systems unless we change our inner systems. Inner excavation in service to this change takes a lot of forgiveness, centering in peace, opening to compassion, and taking right action. Systemic Inner Change is freedom. Freedom from stress, agendas, expectations, separation, and division. Freedom to live in more simplicity, presence, and JOY.

Become a Truth Teller

This is a critical turning point in our collective consciousness. It is time to turn away from our fear-based survival mind to a higher mind that opens us to a deeper connection to our authenticity, our essential natures. Our fears make us live cautiously, carefully, doubtfully, divided and separated from ourselves and each other. When we connect to our truth, we inspire all of humanity to get on with the real work of living in love with ourselves, each other, and our planet. We think we need different solutions for different issues, but by connecting to the JOY within, we expand in every area of our lives.

Healing the Disconnect Within

I spent years of my life punishing myself because I wasn't educated, because I wasn't this and I wasn't that, because my body didn't look like I thought it should look. To hide my feelings of inadequacy, I acted like I was made of iron and steel. I wasn't going to be a burden to anyone. I didn't need anything. I was strong. I had to be in control to keep up the charade of the Avatar.

The world wasn't safe enough for me to be myself. I was intrinsically too different, too weird and too wild. I'm a New York City kid, and I remember when I was little being still free enough to do cartwheels in the middle of a Brooklyn sidewalk, just because I felt like it.

Every time I saw scaffolding (I didn't care what was happening or who was talking to me), I would grab hold of a crossbar, hoist my body up so my stomach was curled over the bar, spin around it, then hop off and keep walking. But as I got older, the more I got messages from society, my caregivers, and everyone who loved me that the Avatar of Grace was more acceptable than the real deal, I capitulated. I began to try harder to please them, to not get in trouble, to not draw too much attention to myself, to follow the rules.

The Grace who didn't have to figure out why she was always in trouble. The Avatar was being programmed to do what it was told.

They were imparting what they felt was love. But really it was a soul prison. The more I pulled those pieces of the real Grace inside, the more I hid, the more I controlled the circumstances of my life, the more I shunned anything that felt risky. Everything that threatened to blow my cover. I became the antagonist of my victim-consciousness story. My body knew I was living a lie before I did and literally started melting down.

Seemingly out of nowhere, my C3 and C4 vertebrae gave out. I had a herniated disc and it extruded, which means that the toothpaste-y stuff sandwiched between the discs popped out. Of course, I ignored the pain and continued to project a strong, capable, eager-to-please front. That's what I was presenting to all, because that was what the Avatar needed to keep little Gracie undercover and safe.

When I realized I really had no clue what to do next, I started diving into change. I started studying change. I started to walk with change. I made change my lover and my breakfast, to see all sides of change and look at change with fresh eyes like I had never experienced IT. And then I sat with little Gracie and felt what she felt about change, how excited she was when the school year was over and summer began, how excited she was when something new was coming. Change was so exciting and delicious when I was a small child. Change only became despicable to me and something to avoid like the plague when I grew up enough to notice the disapproval on the well-meaning faces of my elders and my community at large.

I leaned into the seasons and studied them for their medicine, guidance, wisdom, and counsel. I began to understand that there were cycles of change I could emulate. I could retreat and rest, I could blossom and emerge, I could grow and ascend, and I could mature and evolve. I could die and be reborn. I could feel my Avatar dying, so I knew I needed the offering of rest and retreat that winter provides. Some might view winter as depressing, and others might see winter as a delicious invitation to take a layup day, to stay in bed and rest. But it's hard to relax because our brains are programmed to forever search for something to do.

Our brains often put us in a state of hypervigilance, just like that friend who never knows when to chill or to stop talking. Winter looks inside its closets and says, "I haven't worn that in a long time; out it goes." Winter sheds. Winter examines its friendships and says, "I haven't felt at peace with that human for a while; I will have to say goodbye." Winter looks inside its own heart and says, "I haven't given myself a moment to let go. I will cry and scream; I will release all the rage, pain, and fear I have felt for too long." If you feel your stomach is tight and you are not breathing fully, when with someone or someplace, there's your answer.

I got a little cottage, first place I've ever lived in my adult life completely without children or a partner. I was alone and began to panic, which is a more dramatic and acceptable way to say self-sabotage or hitting my upper limit. We all have a tendency to limit our own happiness because we don't think we deserve for things to go well all the time. These are our upper limits.

Being Present for Your Self

There are moments when we are called to just do nothing but be present, to do nothing but feel into our bodies. Doing nothing, being present, is literally the hardest thing on the planet for me because my love language is learning. I love to unravel, analyze, examine, pick apart; I love to see things differently. What if I turned it this way? Or, well, what if, how do you squeeze that? Or what if I push that thing? I needed to turn that off, to sit in stillness, so my body, my neck, could tell me what it needed to heal, so my heart could speak to me about what it needed to return to JOY.

Being present—what is that? How do we get present? All these books talk about presence. It's such a fancy-seeming concept. What the hell is present? Aren't I present? Aren't I right here in front of you? Present is when you get your brain to be the Sub and not the Dom. We so often perform for each other, which means we're never truly present. If you arrive at a new conversation but you bring with you issues from the past (before this moment), then you are not giving presence its fair opportunity. It's like Spider-Man, flinging those webs out. You fling your webs out . . . you plan . . . and plot. . . . *What am I going to say? What do I think? How am I supposed to act?* We have a tape in our heads all the time. And it feels like another character. That's the duality of us, the yin and yang, the light and dark, the shadows and the luminosity.

BRAIN loves and craves certainty. It observes the world, analyzes behaviors, what you're seeing. Inputs, outputs through a rational knowing built of numbers, data, observations. I observed, therefore X, therefore Y. Proof! When in balance Brain is the structure and support for Heart's Big Dream, the container, in deep intelligence and historical facts, to bring something big to life.

BRAIN IS IQ TO HEART'S EQ.

CFO, COO TO HEART'S CCO, INSPIRING CEO.

A great love told me that praying is speaking to God, and meditation is deeply listening. It's the communication from Spirit to the heart. When do we get time for that if we're not "bored" and alone, right? We look at nature in the wintertime in its most naked, stripped-bare form and it feels uncomfortable because we can feel the echo in our own bodies. The aloneness of nature is startling when you stare into an area of naked trees and brown instead of the lush green landscapes of summer and the blossoming of spring.

There's a void that feels scary if we're allowing our brain to lead. The brain always strives to fill a void, to make sense of emptiness, to distract and invent. The stressed-out nervous system finds the void threatening.

You're in an ultraviolet universe, and being present, rooted, and grounded means that you're fully alive. Experiencing with your ears every sound around you without judgment.

Did you hear it?

Wow.

Harmonics?

In mathematics, a harmonic series describes the divergent infinite series of overtones or harmonics in music. As soon as you say *What is that sound?* you're already out of the experience and back in your head, sliding down the preplanned safety highway. How did I learn how to first stick a toe out, to taking long solo trips into the void?

By one-step-at-a-time-ing it.

Back to using sound as an example. The first step for presence with this sense is to just feel it. Listen with every cell, listen like you have to remember for a test, to impress a potential Lover (whatever visual will motivate you to take your first step).

Hear to translate for all the other senses.

What does the sound feel like in your body?

How does it taste?

Are there any colors to see?

Is there a smell?

Practice that; let every sense be in the present moment.

What are you smelling?

What are you hearing?

Let it cascade over your body.

Notice things softly with your eyes halfway closed. Shapes, colors. The point of inviting all your senses into the experience is to lose YOU in it. Play with it; it's a part of discovering yourself. You are exploring your terrain. Becoming fully present to each gift of the universe IS doing one thing at a time. Soon you'll be able to do it anywhere. Feeling grateful, feeling the glow of Wow, it's a blessing. You're letting heart lead, and the more you lean into heart, you are reconnected to nature as your ultimate teacher, your number-one lover, your ride-or-die, the more you heal, the more you come back to your essential self.

Cultivating Faith

Dr. Martin Luther King Jr. said, "Faith is taking the first step even when you don't see the whole staircase."

Translation: "It's going to be all right, because we are held; we have a team of support everywhere."

In the cottage, during the holidays, I was sick and alone. Craving the feeling of being held, I stretched out in my tub and stared at the trees through the window. They had no leaves, no flowers, no nothing, just nekkid trees. I had never before seen the beauty in that starkness. I'd always avoided places that were cold. I didn't want to feel that message. I wanted to live in the delusion that I could just fake it till I make it. Impossible when you're living authentically, when you are rooted in your ME, when you can say:

I AM, instead of *Am I*?

I let myself feel first in my body what winter felt like. It felt cavernously alone, which scared me. I made up fantastical tales of people coming to get me. Then ego saw an opportunity and asked brain to pull up footage of scare tactics, bad things that happened in the past to scare me back to the ignorant bliss of dependence on anyone | thing outside of myself. Ridiculously hilarious concepts made me have to laugh at myself.

A YOU'RE-WELCOME TOOL

Take a minute to sit or lie down somewhere that feels delicious.

SAY TO YOURSELF "YES" OUT LOUD.

THEN CLOSE YOUR EYES.

VERY SLOWLY BREATHE IN AND OUT.

SENSE INTO YOUR HEART.

MATCH YOUR BREATH WITH YOUR
HEARTBEAT.

If your heart's beating fast, make your inhalations and exhalations longer and longer, taking a pause between each one.

You are using your breath to relax your heart. Loving on and healing yourself.

I was so competitive with myself that I felt like I was failing at breath work.

I couldn't create a flow.

Finally, I heard, "Like in all things, we need a place to rest—even in our breath."

Inhale one, two, three (start with a count of three; don't make yourself crazy) and exhale to three. Bring your belly in completely, make it hollow. . . . It's like your belly button wants to have a make-out session with your spine; pull it all the way in. Then, when you complete the exhalation, feel the pause and regroup before inhaling again. . . .

Learning to make sense of the different parts | characters that are running the business of GRACE. I began looking at existing archetypes and which represents each. While thinking about a phenomenon that's always been in different mediums of art but became highlighted in hip-hop is the hype person.

The one who gets put on, by a big energy and their literal focus in life is being the most entertaining apostrophe or ad lib to the #1's big moment.

EGO in balance is the perfect **HYPE HUMAN.**

As you're continuing to breathe, feel when the belly button wants to meet your spine and let it go all the way there without force. Then, when you inhale, let a full balloon expand in your stomach and then visualize a season. Don't judge it, just see and feel whatever season comes to your mind first.

Okay, you're talking all this big stuff to people about living your dreams and all, but you're scared to death of yours. You're scared of what people will think when you really lean into *Who do you think you are?* And then we echo that new law inside ourselves.

The law of YES and yes.

Stand up straight and look up to the sky.

Put your elbows at your waist, tight to the body with your hands fanning out, making the shape of an uppercase W.

The tempo starts to the pace, rhythm of your heartbeat, and builds through a breath of fire like cadence, like a puppy breathing when excited, and then, with you moving your arms up and down, you rev up to excitement. As your breath crescendos, and as the elbows come down, you allow them to hit your sides (stimulating your side body and kidneys, which activates your sacral and reserve energy stored in your kidneys. It tonifies and promotes blood circuation). Letting your YESSS get louder and fuller with each breath. Staying steady with love for you, energy and flow. Three, two one.

Begin to soften and slow down your YES, allow it to simmer to a soft yes. Juicy and fun to say quieter to yourself, until it's barely a whisper. Keeping the corners of your mouth up and a smile in your eyes. Into a slower, softer, inside energy of Yin Yes. We are locking it in now. Pulling all the alchemy you just created in to simmer, smoldering like the soft, faint smoke of incense. You are stepping into a deep romance with YOU. Feeling delicious as you commune with the magic of you daily. . . . **Secondly**.

Place yourself somewhere in a season that brought you the sensation of JOY. Feel that JOY in your body. Don't judge who was there, what you were wearing; just feel it. If it was a sunny day, feel the warmth on your skin. If it was cold, feel the excitement and the tingling of your body feeling alive. If it was spring, feel how you open up to the sweet newness, like a little kid wanting to skip through a garden looking at all the plants blossoming, unfolding and reminding you of what you missed about them. Spring's like an old friend that you haven't seen in a long time returning and reminding you of just how much JOY, beauty, and bounty there is when you are in communion with nature. If it's summer, skip around, if it's fall, feel the leaves, see the colors on the trees changing. Feel those colors through your body. If you live in a place that doesn't have distinct seasons, visualize a piece of art, a painting or movie, that depicts a season you want to experience.

We sometimes need breaks, just like the seasons. They might blossom in a different way. And you might come back into each other's season at some point, but lean into it. Does your body need a break? Is it time to cleanse? Is it time to take more time to be alone? Is it time to create a space, an incubator to be the container for the seeds that will need to be planted toward the bigger dream for it to start to blossom?

Is it time to recharge from all the excitement that's going to come in other seasons? Could this be the prequel season?

You see where I'm going with this.

When you lean into what each season is about. Is it time to be in the sun and whatever that means, the time to dance more? Is it time to go other places? Is it time to expand? Is it time to take in all the excitement and energy? What do these seasons mean to you? They mean different things to different people, but don't get lost in it because lost and found is a game of the ego, right? It's what can we actually lose that's ours.

Balance and Unity

As time goes on, the more consciousness, the more messages of oneness, unity, JOY, and co-creative solutions to problems you are bringing forward, the more you will be freed in your voice and in your ability to maintain balance in your life. You are going to find that there are more opportunities for service. The work is over. Anything that feels like work or makes you feel angry or makes you feel like *Ugh*, don't do it. You've done the work. You will be helping other people to break through into their consciousness, into their forgiveness, into their peace, and into their freedom by giving them a gateway to come to understanding with themselves on the inside. We'll never be liberated on the outside until we come to peace on the inside. You are going to be educating and serving through JOY. No more martyrdom through suffering. You've been there. This is your era of service through JOY.

During this era where there is a leveling out, where the unsupported by the system(s) of the planet is in a second-by-second dance of perpetual extinction there is a tremendous energy swirl outside ourselves but also within ourselves. If we don't get our shit together and start coming together with co-creative solutions to honor one another, we will not transcend our perpetual pain. Our daily song of complain-bragging about our suffering.

It is time we embody our fave catchphrase of the day—Self Love. Not just as implied but as a devotee of the pleasure of I.

Start treating yourself like you are your own baby. How do you nourish your body, your mind, your soul—so that you can move into deeper balance and flow with the direction our mission requires.

Simplify

Simplify

Simplify

Get lighter in every way

Less stuff weighing us down

Less overhead

Only what makes your HEART light up when you see it, smell it, taste it, and even think about it.

The time we spend playing outside then becomes equal to if not greater than the time we spend on technology and addressing fake things that are designed and curated to addict our lower-vibrating selves. Taking power back starts with loving, caring for, and managing every detail of us, so have a small inventory to make space for magic beyond your wildest dreams.

You get a group of people of all colors, races, nations, who otherwise would be standing on a podium, screaming and pointing fingers. You get them together under the stars at a campfire with drums and dancing—it is amazing how everybody heals. There may be waves that come or rapids that come. They are just vibrations. However, you may be surprised at who you're swimming with. You may be surprised that your fellow swimmer holds you up, and they may not be the people you expected to see in the river. People that you cared about may actually be hanging on to the shore, and you have to allow them to do that with compassion. It's an inner journey.

We cannot get angry at those who do not understand completely where we're coming from. Having compassion and humility is important. You've been mourning the veil of separation from the divine your whole life. What you're looking for is a life of freedom on the inside, where everything is Love, where everything is Peace, where everything is Truth.

Be patient with those who do not understand, just as you have had lives, past lives, and moments in this life, where another held the light for you or you pushed back against the light. Where everybody is in their soul journey and why they do things, the way that they do them—have compassion, not judgment or pity.

Building the TOOLbox—
PLAYING and INVITING JOY into YOUR LIFE

Describe in vivid detail the first time you remember feeling like what you were doing made you totally come alive. What solo activities brought you pure JOY as a child? Was it playing outside? Hula-Hooping? Playing with your dog, riding your bike around the neighborhood? Guess what . . . you can do all those things as an adult. If you loved playing in the dirt as a kid, try getting into a community garden, or (baby steps) . . . buy some houseplants and tend to them lovingly.

I have a ritual when I wake up. Every morning, I dance around in my place, sometimes while Hula-Hooping, and always while blasting my Little Gracie Livin' Life soundtrack. I started when I still had little kids at home, as a way to make mornings more fun. It also was a part of my concept of boot-camping future adults. Teaching them how to start their day with JOY to impact how they felt about themselves and out in the world. Before I reach for my phone or check emails. It has been life-changing. I roll out of bed and straight into JOY.

Reconnect with little you, with what brought you JOY as a child, and bring it back into your grown-up life. I do things every day that fill me with JOY. I stretch or simply roll around on a rug or in the grass. I slow down to appreciate all the beauty and JOY around me. I release through my body, pen, and | or voice all emotions that keep me from feeling JOY. I give all anxiety, restlessness, and looping feelings back to Spirit. I surrender to the light inside me, and I take care of me with the greatest Love that I can muster. From this beautiful state, I trust that I am swimming in an abundance of love, inspiration, and support on all levels.

TOOL

BASKING in LIGHT and LOVE

Sit or lie down, close your eyes, and say out loud, "I am grateful for my angels, guides, guardians, ancestors, animal spirits, crystal spirits . . ." Whatever resonates with you. Each time you express gratitude, feel your heart expanding with gorgeous emerald-green light energy. Nothing to fear. Roadblocks and obstacles magically disappear as you sit in comfort and love, as you come into communion with your own heart.

II

How about Being . . .
a friend among friends . . .
a human in a sea of
rainbow humans.
A lover, loving . . .

The War of the Heart

S peaking generally to shape a concept—we come into this world with huge hearts and the capacity for unself-conscious pleasure as kids; enjoying ourselves was a top priority. Then, over time, we alter ourselves to adjust to other people's expectations. We are now battling with ourselves, never fully appreciating our uniqueness, our unadulterated essence. We are under siege, trapped in perpetual inauthenticity.

Your parents, friends, spouses, exes, bosses, staff, or children don't intentionally diminish you; they believe their doubt and fear-injecting scare tactics are coming from love.

"Exciting that you got a full scholarship to attend Columbia University, but you know you are too timid to live in NY. . . ."

"You can't start your own business; you know it's a _____'s club."

"Only _____ can _____."

"You're too old to _____."

"Too young, etc., etc."

Sadly, I can rattle off tons of these "well-meaning" warnings. When you chisel away the cement of fear that has formed around your heart and crack it open to the freedom of immense JOY, you arrive at your inner knowing. You arrive at the untethered frivolity of your younger self, the self that existed before the judgment and pressure of other people's rules and expectations squashed your Spirit.

When did you start waging war against your heart?

Let's identify and dig into the first moment and the subsequent moments that created the prism of uncertainty you are always battling.

Those moments cascade—and lead to all the Why???s.

"Why can't I find love?"

"Why can't I get the job I want?"

"Why can't I achieve what I want?"

Self-reflection can uncover and has the potential to resolve the subconscious motivations born of conditioning and the projection of fear that have blocked the beautiful feeling of pleasure in your adult body.

THERE'S NO GAME IF YOU DON'T PLAY IT.

How We Unintentionally Choose Small

I was born to high school lovers who got pregnant with me when they were both sixteen years old. A daughter of Irish-Russian-Jewish immigrants, raised in a sheltered household, and rather than being supported, had to find her way alone in a girls' home on Staten Island. Yes, I was born in Staten Island, and raised in Brooklyn. My father is of African slave descent via the South and then the projects in White Plains, New York. My parents were | are both activists, very involved in the local chapter of the Black Panther party when they met. My mother did 78 percent of my rearing. My dad contributed 10 percent when he could. The other 12 percent was made up of my mother's friends, young employees, aunts and uncles, grandparents, etc.

My seventeen-year-old mother did not have it easy. Social Services took me from her as soon as I was born and put me in foster care. Fortunately, my mother had the tenacity to figure out the system and find a job so she could pay for an attorney to get me back. Cementing the lesson for her of what it means to be supported by a system versus not. And through her life mission of extended support, my father's natural leadership ability in any situation, and my paternal grandmother's unapologetic way of living, my inevitable love of service was born.

Service to others is the rent you pay for your room here on Earth.

—MUHAMMAD ALI
FEBRUARY 27, 1978, *TIME* MAGAZINE

The shadow side of that lineage is that it took me making half a lifetime of decisions that didn't acknowledge or support my light to figure out that my habit of playing small was actually learned behavior from infancy. Being VERY general, I feel the way to explain it is . . . safe and well-cared-for newborn babies who know that someone's going to pick them up when they're crying, feed them when they're hungry, and change them when they're soiled are being set up for a life where they can trust that they're at least going to be okay. They grow up with the belief that when they need something, someone will be there to help them. It is safe for them to ask for help, to express their needs, and take up space. They develop the expectation that their needs will be met. They understand that they matter.

Abandoned, neglected, fostered babies, immediately after birth, with no opportunity to bond with their mother or experience connection, love, or a sense of safety, who don't even get a minute to take in the new air now, as they are immediately thrust into the boot camp part of earth school, grow up defensively.

Life began super hard-core from the first second.

Is it okay to be loved? Is it okay for someone to know you? Is it okay to cry? Is it okay to ask for anything? I never wanted to be a problem, a burden to anyone. I wanted to make sure someone was going to come get me, feed me, care for me.

Love ME.

Your early experiences shape you as a child, and in large part determine the conscious and unconscious decisions you make as an adult. It took me a long time to understand why I made the decisions I made. In addition to being in foster care as an infant, I was a mixed-race child, or an "Oreo cookie," a "zebra," as the kids I went to elementary school with referred to me. I had to deal with how to navigate the teasing and found little refuge in my life with my mother, who was perpetually struggling to make enough money to support us. So, to make up for feeling insecure and to not get messed with by other kids, I became the best deep cover. Half the class clown, daredevil, always-fun one with my peers and half the entertaining hostess in everyone's space, the person who was always super helpful and good at counseling and supporting other people.

Hiding in plain sight.

I learned how to give and give and give because that's how I believed I got love and created safety. I didn't feel free to ask for anything: help, love, support, or how to embrace my differences by fully STANDING UP and out in my uniqueness. I had yet to learn the balanced life concept for myself that the duality of Me IS the equanimity of ME. Meaning that I had to grow to stop looking for a limited world to define me, for humans with limited expansive thinking, with a built-in fear to not trust other(s). My love said, *I do not believe that humans believe they have the capacity to be able to understand how two opposing forces can BOTH be TRUE.* I had yet to learn how to allow that truth to just be in ME. To not give in to the world's pressure to squeeze both, all, everything that is me into one tight little box, for others' comfort.

There's a pattern that's created early on that determines how we receive love, how we even look for love, or what we consider to be acceptable love behavior. I was the person who only served to receive love.

In high school, I became the promiscuous one. . . . "Being free," aka trying to find love.

The always-know-where-the-action-is one . . . desperate to keep friends. You get the point.

What personas defined you before you met YOU?

When I was seventeen, I read a book that changed my life. It was a complicated year of super highs and super, super lows. All at once, I had no immediate family in NY, and at the same time I was very deeply in love. AND my career as a chef was taking off. None of it felt like it was planned (that word again ☺).

I began to understand that I could ask for whatever I wanted in life, that I could create the life I wanted based on what I actually felt I deserved. The deserving part was my detour. And that learning to BELIEVE you deserved what you truly wanted was something you had to create for yourself outside of the belief systems handed down to you by your parents and life circumstances. From then on, I became a person who was always looking for something more to learn.

Getting Your Needs Met
by Nourishing Your Soul

When you focus your divine magic on the truth behind the stories you've been programmed to believe, you will find that you begin to be able to manifest what you truly want. And you'll find that it's simple and fun because your desires will not be coming from your mind but your heart and soul. Mind thinks of good ideas and tells you when to go to eat. That's what the mind does. Your mind asks: Is it programmable? Is it data driven? Your power force comes from your Heart and is supported by Spirit.

NO VICTIM CONSCIOUSNESS

Claiming victimhood isn't a road to healing or hope. No matter what happened—no matter how awful the abuse or abandonment—declaring yourself a victim only keeps you victimized. Growth doesn't come from the wrongs that were done to you, but from what you do today, tomorrow, and in the future. We cannot change what happened, but we can take personal responsibility for what comes next. We can change the direction of our internal GPS, and in doing so, we can envision a different and more vibrant future for ourselves.

Wants are always about the mind and ego. The minute you get the want met, there's always another want. A want, for example, is like when you're really hungry for something to nourish you and instead you eat ice cream, and you get high on sugar and then crash. Your sleep is affected and then your next day, etc. It might have felt worth it that time, but that's how wants are. There's always another want, and another want. And it's never satisfying. Needs are nourishing. Needs are a satiating meal. Needs generate from the heart and are based in the soul. They're based in nourishment of the system, whether it's information, clarity, or harmony. Needs come from the inside. It's time to make space for all the new flow coming in.

Place your hand on your heart for a moment.

Take a deep breath and let go of EVERYTHING that has happened prior to this moment.

Let that Light rush through your being.

And then answer these questions from your heart, not your mind.

Are you willing to take a little bit more time each day to listen?

Are you willing to allow your heart to be included in your decision-making processes?

Your body, in order to listen and serve as your chariot, your vessel, needs sleep and good food. Those things can really often sound secondary, but without those things, it will be very difficult to hear your soul. Your ego loves to enslave you to its thoughts, to its control, where no matter what you do, when you're just being in your peace, it's telling you you're not getting stuff done.

You're not doing enough. And then when you are being super busy, it criticizes you. It is tyrannical.

The mind is all about safety, so the mind tends to hook into *Be careful, bad things could happen if you want too much or if you ask for too much.* It's a voice. And there are two voices inside you. Why not let this go? Why not take some time? Why not do this thing that you just really, really want to do? Why not just say, *Screw this, it doesn't serve me.* It's very exciting and very spontaneous. But then there's the other voice. *If I don't get this done right now, I could die.*

Start chronologically recording your own beautiful transformation.

Who are you becoming as you seek JOY?

Are you more self-aware?

Do you love yourself just a little bit more? Do you go easier on yourself?

Do you feel lighter?

We celebrate a baby's birth by documenting every second of their life, and we note their achieved firsts. Why don't we note our own "firsts" as adults?

Have a notebook | pad that's dedicated to recording your progress. If you keep going with this practice of positive self-writing, you will start celebrating yourself—making a BIG DEAL about yourself. And we should all do that—celebration is JOY.

Spend one to three minutes at the end of each day writing and | or drawing what you are proud of yourself for so far today.

Today, for example, I am celebrating that I meditated twice and asked for help on a project I am working on. My past stories—telling myself I was an unwanted burden—made this last point a real win.

TOOL

WRITING to RELEASE EMOTIONS

Take out your ME book and begin releasing emotions through your written words—it's a powerful act. Getting anger, pain, fear, insecurity out of your mind and body and onto the page is a way to break up with it. I used to walk around with a pain script of blame and avoidance; it was easy for me to keep this narrative alive until I began to release it onto paper. Seeing the truth of how the fantastical tales I kept on loop in my brain looked on the page was liberating. I could finally see the negative thought patterns that were keeping me stuck.

Instead of thinking about your laundry list of perceived problems, tasks, and grievances, start to tackle said lists through writing, until your worries become manageable (and they will). Once you release them onto the page, they lose their power and their feelings of enormity.

If you are scared to put your deepest feelings on paper because someone could find it (a parent, a partner, an abuser, etc.), my loves, write it down and burn it. Feverishly (without thinking about it), write about a situation that is causing you pain. The whole situation. How you feel about it. What they said, what you didn't say, what they did. Get ugly, say yucky shit. Write. It. Down. Those negative thoughts are only producing more negativity. It is essential to get off the ride. Out of your body and mind, not causing any further dis-ease. Close your eyes, thank the page for its opportunity for growth, and then do my favorite thing . . . burn that S$%T!!!

TOOL

AFFIRMING and EMPOWERING YOURSELF

We all have different levels of trauma—experiences that pierced our hearts and made it more difficult to open up again. We make our pain story bigger, scarier, and more in control of us than our JOY. To show yourself some love, focus on finding words of affirmation that speak to you or make you reflect. It can be a quote from a book, a takeaway from a conversation, a song lyric, or a poem.

Record yourself saying it. Play it back to yourself for as long as it feels good. When someone we love finally opens up to us, we are present, attentive, and ready to love. And guess what: We deserve the same from ourselves.

Open up to yourself. Allow yourself the space to hear yourself speaking words that ring true for you.

I miss bragging on myself with humans I love and feel safe with. This is what we'd do: We'd each go around in a circle and brag and one-up each other. It was fun. It was like we were supposed to. It was not even a competitive thing, with anyone getting upset. . . . I mean, every once in a while, somebody was a knucklehead and took it too far, of course. But overall, it was just an exercise. I remember always leaving those little moments feeling just a little more puffed up in my chest. And proud of all around me. Even the times when someone got one off on me, taking it like a champ is also the gift of a lesson. Compliment yourself for one thing about you that you are proud of. Really do it. Say it out loud. Say it with confidence. We do this *every day* for other people—but how often do we nourish ourselves with that same energy?

When did you first learn it was not safe to illuminate?

I invite us all to bring bragging back in as a practice. Start with yourself. When you're brushing your teeth or washing your face, just once a day look up in the mirror, look yourself in the eyes.

For a second, look at how beautiful your eyes are (even if all you can come up with is you're grateful that you have eyes that work—that in itself is a gift). Then look at yourself, throw out a brag, and just turn around and walk away. Do that a couple times a week, a couple times a day, a couple times an hour.

You're with a friend and you say, *Let's do a five-minute brag contest for fun.* (Or just one minute if five sounds like too much.) Have the group establish ground rules for this exercise, maybe use a little talking stick or whatever. You know your friends and things can get heated; just figure out together how to design | **create your game**. In all great sports, there are many steps to greatness, and some are seemingly very small. Those simple beginnings, the idea, the intention, the follow-through, the practice, and more. So start with bragging about an authentic great attitude, a sunset, something you allowed yourself to feel.

I love to get to know if it's safe for me to brag with another, if it's safe for me to open my whole heart with them. Leaning even more into my vulnerability.

Sometimes, I do a speak-through-song game. I'll text someone a song and literally the song is exactly what I'm trying to convey. Then they have to respond in song, and we do this until we feel like whatever the conversation's message is now clear and has come to a close with a deeper understanding of _____. It's freeing for me because I speak in music. I think in music, I feel the music, I understand music. I sometimes will even feel so crappy that I'll make a short playlist of all songs that help me see things through a new pair of glasses. I'll sit in the tub and listen to it. And, yes, talk back to it like a therapy session. It is essential to get all those thoughts and things out to make way for bragging.

Start to push aside all the places in us that were shamed for feeling good about ourselves. That were made to feel that we weren't good people, that we were selfish, or egomaniacs and full of ourselves when we just stood up a little taller or explored a little bit more than others felt safe. Let's start bragging and find our own words. It doesn't have to be anything that doesn't land for you. The second step of that, when you get good at it: Start recording some of those brags in your phone and listening to yourself sometimes when you're outside and you're working out or walking. Start hearing yourself in your own voice, which is very powerful, because it speaks directly to every cell in your body.

TOOL

BEING GENTLE with YOURSELF

I vow from this moment on to be gentle with myself. To accept myself, to appreciate where I have been and what I had to work with, for in this moment I can make positive use of it all. I choose to fully and graciously live life as it comes. I believe the richest rewards, by far, come when I sincerely give of myself. A simple promise: I vow from this moment on to be gentle with myself.

*Trust you are attempting one
of the defining moments
of your life,
courageously drawing
love that is eternal to you,
and the healing that has
been lifetimes in the making.*

Architecting a Life of Being Wanted

L ittle Gracie wanted to be wanted by others. She created an entire life of service to acquire love. Being in that deep cover inside this Avatar I built to live and survive missioning.

To keep my life certain, to keep my cover from being blown, I lived in deep control of everything. Deep control of every second, and we all know what a big joke that is, since in truth, we can't control anything. I lived by analyzing every detail, every second. I am tired just saying that. All strategy was with brain, fueled by ego. Heart was completely pushed out, abandoned by me. I ignored her and treated her like an old friend who only gave me bad advice, and leaned into the smarter, more strategic, clear, "how the 'real world' works" brain to drive the ship, with ego balancing things in the right way for my successing, copiloting.

When I worked in entertainment, I always felt differently when I worked at a company led by a creative versus a company led by a much more business-minded human being. I am not judging either, but what a different experience it was to be in a space where the creativity led with room for spontaneity. The collaboration and the passion of multiple concepts emerging for the enjoyment of a shared experience, versus a company led by a more business-minded human. A company led by data, focus groups, and analyzing, and therefore the creativity had to fit into the strategy built from the facts.

We've all experienced things that were a lightning-in-a-bottle success or hit. One experience felt by everyone at the same time and then fizzling out, never to be seen or heard from | about again. Those kinds of mass experiences are often hard to predict. That phenomenon in my professional career in a creative space helped me untangle and understand how I operated in my life so JOYlessly.

Architecting success, succeeding, and being wanted. Over living soulfully, passionately in love with my own imperfect being and DEEPLY InJOY. Illuminating brightly while getting to play with other humans, who also are on their missions on earth school.

The call guided by spirit to daily, secondly embody Love and Grace.

For Grace to practice Grace.

To every day be in integrity with how I communicate, inspire, and instigate others to feel in JOY as my life's mission and work.

Once again, when I get out of the way of myself, I am awarded a life and reality beyond my wildest dreams. This was all completely opposite of how I was living my day-to-day. A traitor to my now-known mission. My own belief to control every situation around me so I didn't feel anything deeply enough to not be able to be in control of the relationships around me, which were all a part of my life to succeed in the bigger dream. And why that never felt icky or transactional or bizarre in my day-to-day life versus how I'm writing and reading it to myself and you're reading it right now. I always had a mission to live at least with integrity and respect myself and any breathing thing I come in contact with, so it always felt like my mission was good for everyone. I justified to myself . . . I am a GOOD person.

All of us build Mission Statements for our Avatars, which become our Bibles, filled with false scripture that ultimately has nothing to do with who we are or what we believe in our hearts. Let's explore how we end up building personalities and even entire lives based on what we think others want from us. All the things that keep us disconnected from the truth that we are always connected to Spirit.

The Spirit Within Us

We're not taught early on how to deal with the full rainbow and range of emotions. Without really clear, strong, aware humans to guide us, we begin to believe that the heart is a dangerous place. That when we feel from the heart, we experience pain. We learn to do whatever we must to avoid pain. Pain is such a confusing and misunderstood feeling. However, it serves as an instigator, a poke, to move us out of our current situation, or to push us to look deeper into our feelings, or to explore what's uncomfortable.

Daring to Open Your Heart

It's the summertime, school's out, and you are being sent somewhere for the summer that you're very nervous about. The great unknown. You just got into a good groove of making friends, feeling like your life is going the way you want it to go. And you get to this new place and you're hanging out and it's fun, but you see it's very cliquey, and it feels hard for the first few weeks. You feel weird. You don't know who to talk to. You have to explain yourself all the time. It's an uncomfortable situation, and every night you pray for one friend, one friend. If you could figure it out, break the code, and get one friend, this whole summer experience would be different, and you could shine, and then all the expectations you had for this particular summer would come true.

Then it happens! You meet this person. You click immediately. Finishing each other's sentences. You love the same movies. You love the same food. You want to do the same things. You have the same excitement about things. It's just perfect. But instead of enjoying this friendship, all of a sudden, all of the focus, all of this big energy that you're putting on the wanting of, the manifesting of this great friendship, is now focused on not losing the friendship. So instead of being present in it, it's just this constant running loop of losing the friendship, everything that's a threat to the friendship. There are a million words for this concept of just choking the shit out of something that brought a lot of JOY at one point and then is all of a sudden not fun for anyone, even your other friends, when it could have been an opportunity to make new friends or to expand your social circle and have new experiences. All of a sudden, they're a threat, so you're the one on the outside, and everything becomes an issue of *them and us* and how much time you get. And all of a sudden, even the friendship becomes complicated to the friend because it's not what that person signed up for.

When artists have that first big dream and they're hungry and they're excited about what they are creating, they put so much energy into proving, manifesting, making, ideating, and creating, just making this first thing happen. Once the magic _____ is revealed, the focus shifts to holding on to it so tight that they squeeze the crap out of it.

Then often the next phase is reworking it a million times instead of being openhearted and fearless in the acquisition of the next dream. Not opening to what's next.

We all do this with so many things we love.

We splurge on something we see: I love it!!! Bought it and am bringing it home. . . .

But before we can enjoy it, we say: Don't touch, it's only for special occasions, not for us. It's for others.

Wanting something, loving it, seeing it, it bringing you JOY in that moment, and then making sure you hide it away so that nothing happens to it so it's always there, bypassing the complete moment of the JOY and the excitement and the gift itself. I'm noticing this more and more in this season we're in. It's a real duality of wanting extreme freedom and understanding the benefit of being the bee and spreading the pollen, if you will, spreading the energy. And I don't even mean sexual, just intimate energy or heart-sharing energy in spaces where we inspire each other to grow and muse each other into our best emanation of our big light selves. But instead we literally put a giant-ass lampshade over things and squash them to death.

What Needs to Shift Inside?

If we all felt immense JOY and security from our love being rooted within, we would unite, support, and see each other as unique gifts. We would be a revolution of JOY. This is the first day of the rest of your life. Find your birthday number and circle it. Draw your happiest face. These are tools. Play your eleven-year-old self's favorite song. Sing like crazy. Be the life partner you want to attract. LOL.

Begin to see, understand, and take action to stop sabotaging and dismissing your gifts. A firm no is a gateway drug to a life-evolving yes. Luck is what people say they need when they don't want to own their power. Going back to your own life school to feel the consequences of what you're feeling, master life skills. The science of achievement, how to manifest it. The art of fulfillment, the quality of our life, is based on the quality of our emotions. All of us have emotional homes. The place we always go back to. The goal is to have an extraordinary life always. Success without fulfillment is the ultimate failure.

Ask yourself: Why did I come here? My answer: I am here to transform my life into JOY, to release all fear and doubt, and smallness of old Grace. Living in love deeply with myself and not in perfectionism, but in deep curiosity for its own unfolding.

Bring compassion back to people. The more harshly we judge each other, the more harshly we judge ourselves. A leader doesn't fit into a culture. A leader creates their own culture. Drowning in information but starving for wisdom.

Meaning equals emotion; emotion equals life. Get out of emotions of the past. The strongest force in any personality is the need to stay consistent with how we define ourselves.

Not Laughing Is No Laughing Matter

The fact that play is good for you, that it's productive and inspiring, is hardly new news. Pick up any business magazine and you'll see that famous corporate leaders, artists, inventors, and entrepreneurs have all integrated play into the workday—try finding a tech company without a Ping-Pong table in the office. And just as play is clearly worth the investment for corporations, it's worth the investment for YOU, too. Your JOY is serious business, and every business needs a strategy to grow.

That's where I come in as a JOY Strategist. No, I don't bustle around picking out JOYs for people like a Personal

JOY Shopper. What I do is offer strategies to facilitate the search. Mostly, I remind people about what they've always known—that you can find JOY through play. You've got to identify JOY for yourself. All I support is finding your way. I, too, have gone to my fair share of healers, therapists, and life coaches, and all of them have been helpful to some degree or another—but what all of us need to do is look inward. To look inward is to recognize that you're your number-one boss; you're the coach you most want to please. To look inward is to find your JOY—which is really your own personal guiding star. Once we discover JOY, we've scored a GPS that can get us anywhere—our inner guide.

I'm here to light you up on the inside—to supercharge your inner guiding star. If you came over to my house, I might greet you at the door with fun stuff and then walk you around to decide what to play with first. Or to design your dream city out of candy-colored building blocks. But since you're not coming over, I'm just going to remind you about some shit you already know but forgot . . . PLAY.

Good Mornings Start Here

Think about it this way. Every day when you wake up, you have a decision to make:

How do you want to feel today? If you start each day with an experience of JOY, you connect to your heart and imagination. If you start the day that way—in touch with your JOY, your truth, your desires—you're going to be able to run your day instead of having your day run you.

Everybody has their own sources of JOY, and everybody has to discover and rediscover them on their own, but one of the most important things every single one of us needs to do is figure out a practice to start the day that does not involve waking up and grabbing your phone. Start with yourself first—not your phone. Don't even start with your partner, your dog, your kids, your boss. Even if it's one minute of listing things in your mind that you're grateful for as you lie in bed (it can be as simple as *I'm grateful I woke up today and I'm here on this earth*), you do YOU first. Period.

I dance wildly to my favorite music with no judgment about how I look, right when I roll out of bed. It's a game changer to my more sluggish days.

TOOL

The DANCE of THANK YOU

When you feel at your complete wit's end, when your body is tight, not breathing in your belly, not fully open in your chest, that's always my indication to move slower. When my stomach is tight and my chest is tight and I'm not breathing the full bottom to top, I start a mantra of *Thank you*. Just *Thank you*. *Thank you*. *Thank you*. Say it in different tones, *Thank you*, and then whisper, *Thank you*. *Hi, thank you*, and just keep changing the ranges of *Thank you* so it hits every part of your body and everything around you. Just sing it like a song or say it, march it, dance around it. Let yourself be enveloped in *Thank yous*. And then when you feel your body start to soften, breathe a very long, deep breath, say one cosmic *Thank you* to everything and all there is, to all the teams and all the support around you. Take another deep breath for yourself for taking care of yourself, and get back to life as it is.

TOOL

ILLUMINATING ENERGY

For your immediate healing: Inside you is a packet of golden energy. . . . Please breathe in and connect with it and use this as a healing energy drip today. Think of it like an IV going into your veins except this is going into all your energy bodies. It radiates from your center, filling every space, starting with your physical at the cellular level and moving to the spaces between the spaces. It flows to your emotional, mental, spiritual, and abundance bodies where you manifest well-being and love.

IV

*When JOY impacts JOY,
it is LOVE.*

:)

Rock
or
Disco

I n the fifth grade, it was the thing to do in new situations—first day of school, church, with new kids on your block, summer camp, etc.—to figure out as quickly as possible if they were YOUR people or not. The method du jour was . . . looking someone directly in the eyes and asking | challenging them with THE question . . .

"Rock or disco?"

I know it sounds ridiculous, but this really was the sorting process for great relationships in 1981. I'd been trying to figure out who or what I actually was, because I couldn't see myself reflected in anything or anyone around me. On the first day of fifth grade, when some kid walked up to me and asked, "Rock or disco?" I felt in my body that this was the right moment for me to define myself as someone with more colors, more dimensions. I loved to wear my rainbow suspenders over my white-and-purple baseball shirt. That was my favorite outfit. Oh yes, I also loved to weave a purple ribbon through my side ponytail braid! This "rock or disco" moment was going to be my defining moment. For the first time, I was going to be able to communicate who I really was, who I felt I was inside. I boldly faced this kid and answered, "I don't just like rock, and I don't just like disco; I like them both equally." I remember feeling so much pride, taller, like my spine straightened a bit and my shoulders rolled back as I puffed my rainbow-suspendered chest out ever so slightly.

I had yet to learn that I am music; we all are.

The first time I bought a couple of albums with my allowance, I remember loving and savoring the covers. You could make a mobile from the insert in the Stylistics' album, and the Grease soundtrack album was a double-sided yearbook. I poured myself into these other worlds. I felt like I belonged, and in my excitement, I felt a connection from the first note. I loved a wide variety of music and felt it all so deeply. That really began to make me feel that who I was wasn't disgusting, weird, or unacceptable. Listening to all the different music I loved made me feel that I was actually more interesting than the people who sided with this or that. The people who claimed that I had to identify as one thing or another to really belong.

In spite of how my childhood sounds on paper and how truly painful a lot of my early experiences were, it is clear to me how they were necessary to shape the messages in the learnings. The education I needed to experience to be a person serving through the gift of JOY. When I play the collection of songs that are my life thus far, I stop and lean into the feelings of certain memories. Some bite, some burn, some leave a scar, and others create the character I lead with today, but all together they are one immense feeling . . . With nothing else to compare to I appreciate and have grown to love my whole childhood. I had so many moments to be in gratitude for what I just didn't understand were difficult at the time. We moved around a lot, my mother always bringing me into different circles of fascinating people, doing their version of brightening up the planet. My curious excitement for all things I don't know yet was a very helpful skill since I met someone new often. I find it funny how we scavenger-hunt through life, picking up little clues that lead to more clues. Finally graduating to a new level of seeing the Game, the world, higher consciousness. So, you have new tools to play the next level of the game and so on and so on. . . .

My father's family, regardless of if he was physically present or not, was a whole 'nother set of traditions, ideas, philosophies, and ways of playin' the game—all of them brilliant and fascinating. I soaked it all up, as if every moment was a part of a giant miniseries. It was dangerous to stare at people in the early '80s, though, so I learned to be covert about my intense excitement to hear people's stories. But being a human who loves nothing more than to learn through hearing and | or experiencing another, I love to grow by being on the ride, visualizing in my head while I look deeply into their eyes for their feelings and other clues in tidbits I may get to expand the version of the story I was literally creating inside my head as they spoke.

So you see why there really was no better life for me to choose to jump into. Inside a human experience, craving being and giving love. Desiring to have even a morsel of connection with everyone around me. To be for a second inside their experience, to feel their story. That no matter who they are, I feel deeply privileged and honored that they would trust me with it. So of course my Boot Camp would be a giant soup of -isms. With wild and unbelievable opportunities, in terms of creating a life list of which ingredients to pick for the perfect Grace recipe.

These days I find it challenging to impossible to tell another's age, socioeconomic reality, and sometimes gender identity from the way they look on the outside. The don't judge a book by its cover concept is realer than ever. Or at least we are now collectively more open to different stories around it.

If I knew before age ten that the perception through your outward appearance would no longer be one of the leading factors of adult success, I would not have allowed it to bring me such sorrow. A child in the '70s, being social and chosen had a lot to do with what it looked like you could afford. You either came from something that completely benefited from the system, with more resources than anyone would ever need for at least four generations. You were someone who felt entitled to play and stretch out, to claim, to dream. To pioneer with complete confidence that they would always be supported living out your goals, no matter how big the mission.

Or people who may have a lot of family love, traditions, but whose main focus for survival is making sure they are a part of the established community to feel safe. Often with few resources and therefore not supported to believe in individual dreams. And it was very obvious to tell which was which based on what symbology of status you could afford. The simplicity of entertainment options made the marketing to have more, more intense. There were only a few channels on TV and very few stores that catered to a budget-minded consumer. As a kid I learned early that my life's goal was to at least look like I could afford to look like I was a part of Group A. But I feared that I had no chance of ever advancing to Group A. Most of my clothing came from secondhand stores. The older I got, the more clearly I could even see the business strategy. Group A stayed in the top-tier position by selling, marketing, and propagandizing so that Group B would keep spending their wee resources to aspire to Group A's status. All this to say how heavily feeling poor impacted my desperation to always be different than I was as a kid. To shake all the lesser-than aspects of myself to belong.

My family and friends continued to ask strange questions that indicated that they thought I was some kind of an alien. I had felt like I had to downplay my creative, colorful side all the time, just to make them feel comfortable. It was such a bizarre double life. It became clear to me very early that if I wanted to be accepted, if I wanted to make people comfortable, I had to show up as what that particular community, family member, friend expected. Around that time, I started to notice that the conversations from well-meaning adults shifted from "How was school?" to "What do you want to be when you grow up?" That concept was always a strange one. I remember feeling puzzled in my soul anytime anyone asked me that. It's not something I ever thought about. I always just thought about what was right in front of me, what I was going to tackle with every single thing inside me, everywhere around me. It wasn't that I wanted to do or be anything specifically. It was an entire experience that always shifted me. If I felt an entire experience that then felt aligned to me in a way I never felt before, I did all the things to shift into that experience of myself. I deep-covered, over and over again, to feel it. When adults would say, "What do you want to be when you grow up?" I just remember looking at whoever asked me and analyzing if their particular life was what I wanted to experience as a "grown-up" or not. I started feeling into what I actually did want. What I came up with was that I wanted to do something to change the world. I had no idea how I would do that.

I got glimpses of pieces of the bigger puzzle for my future self when I experienced Madame Zenobia's character in *Uptown Saturday Night*, Marlon Brando's character in the first *Godfather* movie, Mister Rogers, *Pee-wee's Playhouse*, *Mad* magazine, Pink Floyd's *The Wall*, Tracey Ullman, Robin Byrd, Blondie, Bad Brains, Minnie Riperton, and all of the moments I felt in my soul were the beginning of my journey back to my true self and an amalgamation of the seeds of my mission on earth school. They all challenged the collective us to see how to wield change and most importantly taught me that my contrarian spirit IS my gift.

Music saved me. I didn't have the words or language for it when I was young, but nothing turned (and still turns) me on more than creativity and brilliance in music. That "rock or disco" moment gave me permission to lean into all of it. I hung out with all creatives and misfits—a motley crew of kids, we played together in Washington Square, Tompkins Square, Prospect, and Central Parks, depending on the day. When I was a little older, we'd all hang out at clubs like Danceteria or CBGB's Sunday hard-core matinee. I loved going to the reggae lounge and Hotel Amazon. It was ALL so fun to me.

However, nothing was more exciting than what was beginning to emerge around me—a movement, a revolution, a new way of communicating, a new culture, the new language of hip-hop. I started to meet the architects of that new scene, and when we met for the first time—each one in different scenarios as they were building their now-illustrious careers—we just had to look each other in the eyes to know immediately . . .

YES, of course, it was rock AND disco.

Even Tinker Bell Needs Boundaries

As I got older, I took on more and more responsibilities and had less time at my disposal, and I've had to face the challenge of learning to create boundaries and make hard choices. Choosing rock and disco as a kid allowed me to begin to be all of who I am, to stand out proudly in my rainbow-colored suspenders, but it also created a dilemma. I had to learn to prioritize, so that I could do the things I really wanted to do. Not easy! In the last few months there has been a surge of interesting people appearing in my life and different opportunities being offered to me. I can feel little Gracie wanting to reject this surge. As a child I was a hummingbird, happily Tinker Bell–ing around the world, loving everybody and wanting to experience everything. The downside of this was that I would inadvertently hurt people's feelings because I would make too many overlapping plans and then certain people would inevitably be let down when I couldn't attend to everything I'd committed to. The fallout of that behavior, of not wanting to choose one thing over another, of wanting to do everything all at once, meant that I had to manage a lot of relationships and soothe a lot of heartbreak. When I was a young adult, my solution was to try to alter myself by being less social, to do what other people did. Like having only one best friend, or one community. It seemed that you were supposed to live in one neighborhood where you have your people, your local support. You were supposed to marry one person and stay in one place. I tried to conform to this concept of limitation rather than experiencing life as a giant cuddle puddle, which is really how I want to live. I love the deliciousness of layering ideas, souls, people, energies, nationalities, and cultures. This approach makes the most delicious pot of fun that turns into lessons, growth, learning, and illumination. I tried the life of conformity for a while, but it never felt integral to my authentic self. It felt like such a colonizer concept, this idea that there is one correct way to live life. The need to identify as one thing made me feel like the person I am is inherently wrong because I come from people of two different races/nationalities and multiple different cultures. In the '70s, '80s, and '90s in New York, everybody was striving for whatever was purebred. *I'm a hundred percent from this place. It's a hundred percent all of that.* A lot of the marketing at that time was about being solidly one thing. It was best if your flag was one color and your ideas boiled down to one concept. Eventually, I landed in a community of interesting people, and it seemed that all my dreams were coming true. But what's funny about getting married, having children, and becoming part of a community is that it triggered all the reasons I had to start rejecting the marketing I had allowed myself to buy into IN THE FIRST PLACE. The persona that I believed was who I was. That life temporarily turned me into a very secretive, overly private person who was not open to different experiences. When I am single, I always feel so fantastic, free, and alive. I have new adventures and travel to different places. As soon as I was in a deep partnership, I felt like I had to change to merge and deliver the Grace I believed they wanted, and that created resentment.

There you go . . . it makes perfect sense that all my relationships and my deep partnerships and marriages, and even trying to be a lifer at certain companies and stay a long time, always failed because at my essence I am not that. I am much more like a bee going from flower to flower. I pick up the delicious pollen and then I continue to move around the world and flower, and blossom, and plant and grow things. When I'm living in that consciousness, I feel so alive. It's such an interesting thing that I've chosen to spend so many years of my life not being that. Even sexually, even with religion and spirituality, I really enjoy the melting pot of many layered experiences.

I started my journey after my last divorce learning to say NO, because I was a people pleaser. I said yes to everyone, and yes to everyone else's experience in order to help them grow. I lost myself in that completely because I had lost sight of who I really was. Before I learned to say NO, I was demonizing myself for not being able to conform to the big dream. The one partner, the one best friend, the one community, the one job, or the one business or the one . . .

However, after learning to say NO and finally getting to be comfortable with prioritizing myself, a deep heart-opening book helped me start saying YES again and allowing myself to figure out my personal rules around YES and NO along the way. What's interesting is that I'm butting up against this thing now where I haven't figured out my personal rules around that. How I enlist the boundaries that help me take the time to gestate, to form, to grow, and eventually to blossom. When a seed is in the ground, you can't see it gestate and form itself into what it will eventually blossom into. You can't see if you like the way it's growing before you invest in creating an entire garden. You can't know if that one seed is developing in a way that will please you. You don't know before it has flowered if you will love the way it looks, feels, and smells. Maybe learning to create boundaries that answer all my needs, that allow me to figure out how to integrate all of who I am, the multicultural rainbow that is the expression of who I am, takes time. Maybe it's about looking to nature again and seeing the cycles, the seasons. Maybe I can't jump into anything with anybody professionally or personally until I've allowed for a ten-month gestation cycle to complete. Maybe it will take an entire year before I can see how the first few months of the birth will work out before we actually decide to get married or go into partnership and build something bigger together.

I'm sitting here with a lot of things to untangle and wanting to figure out from a much higher consciousness how to support Grace in feeling alive and excited every day.

Valuing Your Story

I had a lot of excuses for staying small. I'm a behind-the-scenes person. I always bragged that I got promoted many, many times but never had a trade photo taken of myself because it wasn't about me. Or . . . when someone's accomplishments were at least in part due to my efforts, support, and creativity, I never wanted to be the person to stand up and say that I had anything to do with it. Taking credit was not my strong suit or what I thought was important. It was suggested I stop hiding from the camera. "You're erasing yourself from history" was the direct statement. That's when the value of taking credit when it's due really hit me! When you're dating someone new, you go out of your way to make them feel special. Do that for yourself . . . every single day. Start your day by thanking yourself for something beautiful or responsible or kind or hard you did. I don't care if it's "I'm so proud of you for being so responsible and for caring so much for your own work. I know you were tired, and it was cold outside, but you got up, got dressed, got out of the house early, parked your car a mile away because there was no parking close by, and made it to that important meeting on time!" or "I'm so proud of you for continuing to try to kick coffee. And you're doing it!" or "I acknowledge you for having tea this morning!" You must start patting your own self on the back. You'll be surprised by how good acknowledging and thanking yourself makes you feel about yourself.

Your *You're Welcomes*

We live in such an incredible time when our options are almost limitless. What spiritual faith or religion do you want to practice? What do you want to study? What do you want to know? Who do you want to be? What do you want to wear? How do you want to wear your hair? Where do you want to work? What kind of work do you want to do? Who do you want to date? Who do you want to screw? Who do you want to play with? What kind of music do you want to listen to? What movies do you like to watch? Where do you want to travel? Where do you want to live? Who do you want to meet? What do you want to eat?

I love that there are also so many options for healing our bodies and minds, but even that can become overwhelming. It can become economically challenging. So . . . how do we truly support our health and well-being if we are in the business of taking great care of our vessels so they last for a long time? If we're committed to living in service to true self-love, if we're dedicated to living every second in the juiciest way possible, how do we support ourselves?

What songs, sounds, rituals, prayers, and meditations deeply address your own soul's needs? How do you commune with your beloved in every moment? What would that look like?

What could you provide for yourself that your body and soul would thank you for? Every single time I dance or laugh, read or take a walk, I hear my heart saying, *Thank you.* What are your *YOU'RE WELCOME*s?

TOOL

CULTURAL REF GAME

What are THE influences that shaped who you are today?

Grace's Fifty-Plus-Year INFLUENCES . . .

MUSIC: As a verb, adjective, friend, teacher, instigator, lover . . .

MY MAGIC CHILDREN: In all the ways

ART: In all its expressions and emotions

PLAYING IN WATER: Canoeing, floating, swimming, etc.

SESAME STREET + THE ELECTRIC COMPANY + THE MAGIC GARDEN

COMING TO AMERICA

THE CONCEPT OF ROSEBUD BEING THE SLED–the simple JOY in a complicated life

THE NATIVE TONGUES

DR. MAYA ANGELOU

MINNIE RIPERTON + PRINCE + BLONDIE

MADAME ZENOBIA FROM *UPTOWN SATURDAY NIGHT*

LISA BONET

MAD MAGAZINE

MISTER ROGERS + CAROL BURNETT

THE ROBIN BYRD SHOW + THE TRACEY ULLMAN SHOW

TOOL

I AM

When I am not completely rooted in my I AM . . .

I represent as . . . AM I?

I visualize that state as the cans attached to the back of a wedding car. Dangling on the road, getting bumped around and making noise, but they're not really a part of the experience and are clearly not having a good time.

Sit or stand, whatever's comfortable for you. Take a deep breath. . . . As you inhale, feel a warm, bright, beautiful light coming up from Earth's center, and as you draw that energy up though your feet and legs, feel it ignite the fire in your perineum, the area between your booty and your genitals, also known as your root chakra. As you exhale, release all the tension from your body.

As you practice this centering and activating breathing exercise, ask yourself, "What is my I AM?"

Do you think/say:

"I AM a great parent."

"I AM a wonderful friend."

I would encourage you to choose a different path. Those two examples are about how you serve others. (See how tricky this is?)

Try instead:

"I AM lovable, loving, love itself."

"I AM creative, adventurous, generous of spirit. . . ."

"I AM powerful, beautiful, connected to all there is. . . ."

Once you've created your list of I AMs, I recommend that you do the next exercise on a daily basis for as many days/weeks/months/years as it takes for you to wholeheartedly believe what you've written on your list.

After a few rounds of root chakra breathing, stand in front of a mirror and speak your list out loud with confidence while gazing lovingly into your own eyes. For each I AM that you have a hard time saying, repeat it three or more times until it begins to feel natural.

V

Don't ever think I fell for you,
or fell over you.
I didn't fall in love,
I rose in it.

—TONI MORRISON, *JAZZ*

Are You My Lover? Guru? Teacher? Are You My HOME?

I feel like my whole life has been about trying to figure out who or WHAT I am. As a child, I couldn't see reflected in anything around me who or what I might be. I kept going deeper into finding love and pleasure—outside of myself. I hadn't "gone in" yet. Instead, I went from person to person, looking for them to fill me up. I was giving myself away. I made other people my happiness—lovers, spouses, friends. I was in a forty-year battle to find love. Locating your happiness in and through other people is a surefire path to unhappiness.

Off the Love Hamster Wheel

When I was a child, I loved reading the children's book *Are You My Mother?* I read it many times to my children when they were little, but it took me a long time to figure out why I loved it so much when I was a child. That is, until I set out on this incredible journey inward of writing this book. I realized that I could connect to the experience of the baby bird falling out of the nest. I feel I've lived my life constantly asking these questions: Are you my family? Are you my lover? Are you my opportunity to connect, to find my family, to feel safe? Are you going to provide me with that that big illuminating certainty that we humans look to as our North Star?

That book showed me something I couldn't see until now. Instead of just relaxing in my body and connecting to life from a present open place, I was constantly running through life foraging or hunting for something else, always trying to figure it out. And then resting for a second at the top of that very low peak, until I propelled myself back out into my valley, still without understanding that the present is NOT about settling into uncertainty and discomfort, but about settling into and enjoying those very high valleys and those low peaks. The love hamster wheel I couldn't seem to jump off until I was hit in a place I didn't even know needed help. As I've said many times, everything is everything. And yet, for this big lesson, which at the time just felt like, *How did I miss that?* I always felt I had incredible, solid friendships that were outside of whatever complications I was having in my core family. My friends, my chosen family, they always held me down and vice versa. It was one place I could be myself and feel safe.

I leaned hard into a friendship that started to feel identical to my long, complicated, intimate love journeys with all the Loves in my life. Seeing that giant web of emotions over things that I care so deeply about, in a way that I had to address it. I had to step back and understand why now I had to question everything, why I was being forced to change in areas that my ego felt we were done with, that we felt we had the gold stars for. At this older passage of my life, I got to the point where I found a new thing to beat myself up with, which is: *Have you really made your life's mission about finding a life partner?* And that answer is no. It's about that love, that love that I now feel on so many levels viscerally, just as I breathe and look at the sun, and stretch out my toes in grass, and hear laughter, starting with my own. Just living in the living of life, not the doing of life, not the getting of life, not the winning of life, but just the being in life.

The Ultimate Love Story

When it comes to love, we're taught to look for a special someone who's out there searching the globe to find us and to make life magical as we're drawn together with a charge powerful enough to keep planets in orbit. I thought I'd found this once, twice, three times. +.

I took on relationship after relationship—eagerly—like a student determined to earn a master's degree in Partner Love. Once the last one crumbled in my arms, I questioned not just the partners but the overall mission.

In some part of my brain, I understood that there was no Prince Charming—and I also didn't think I needed a _____ Charming. I was strong, I was proud, I was independent. I had a great career and incredible children, but I still wondered how it was possible that I could achieve ownership in so many areas of my life, but never really hold on to real estate in the area of love.

I needed to turn my attention inward, not outward. Get a load of that: Our inner guide—our North Star—can also guide us to love. Falling in love with ME.

The being right there in the bathroom mirror! Who was she? What was she like? I'd seen who she was around a group of people, but who was she when she was all alone?

It finally occurred to me that I might do better going forward if I took a minute to take stock of where I'd been.

Multiple husbands.

Affairs.

Bankruptcy.

A cornucopia of abuses.

A lack of value incoming and outgoing.

Or, wait a minute, was it possible that I was the one who just didn't see my own value? Is that how I presented myself to the world? As someone of little value who largely existed to promote the value of others? I just had to wonder: Were all these botched relationships just reflecting how I felt about myself?

Or had I deliberately downplayed myself, playing it safe by holding myself back from blossoming to my full potential?

Dating Myself

Have you ever thought about the cumulative amount of time you've spent getting to know a new lover?

Who are you really?

What do you most want out of life?

I couldn't count how many times I'd sat fascinated at the edge of my seat, tirelessly asking them questions and loving it as they went on and on. I had a knack for asking questions that encouraged my dates to reveal all their beguiling facets—but I had no idea how I'd answer such questions myself.

If asked.

I was destined to spend the rest of my life with myself—I needed to understand who the hell I was signing up for. Who was I? What did I enjoy?

This is when I began my life-changing exploration of JOY. What brought me JOY? Like most people, I had no idea, but I started asking myself the sort of questions I'd probably ask a lover if I were out to plan a surprise party for this person—except the party I was planning was for me, and I wanted it every day of my life.

As I've mentioned, discovering each thing that gave me JOY was a life-changing revelation. Every time I'd give in to JOY, I'd drown out all the dooming, downer voices in my head that I'd never realized had hijacked my life. I'd start each day with JOY—dancing, singing, doodling—doing anything I love—without these voices droning on and on, editing my desires and my sense of what I deserved.

Some of the nastiest and most paralyzing notions that rattled around my head weren't issued by Society or Culture or the world's unwritten rules. The nastiest and most paralyzing noise came from all the mean things I said to myself. *Grace, you sure f$%ked up again! Oh, Grace, you'll never learn!*

I quickly realized that if I was going to date myself, I had to put in the effort to be a kind and good-hearted lover—just like I would be if I were dating anyone else. I had to romance myself. Rather than beating myself with admonishment, I had to sweet-talk myself instead. *Look at you! You've got this, Grace. You really are Amazing.*

Instead of trudging through the days of my new/renewed divorce life and falling miserably into bed each night, I turned on the charm and started courting the hell out of myself.

And why not? I'd done it for everyone else I'd ever dated! Kicking off each morning with a ritual of JOY set the stage for living each day like it was a love letter to myself—and every night was a date night for me, myself, and I.

Seriously, Grace, date night with yourself? You don't have time for this. (Hello, self-sabotage!)

But then I would think: *How much time have I given to other people? How many hours did I miraculously find time to get lovey-dovey at the start of any other relationship?* I had the time. I'd make the time, because I was giving myself the hours that I'd always seemed to find for everyone else.

TOOL

TURNING Yourself ON

Are you doing enough to be a great partner to yourself? Make your bedtime SEXY, especially if you are alone. Wear something soft to the touch, something that reminds you of your sexiness. Or wear nothing at all.

Re-create and redecorate your bedroom, shower, bath, and dressing space(s) in your physical home just for your own pleasure.

TOOL

TOUCH It, IT'S Yours

Lie down somewhere very comfortable, a spot where you're not looking at anything you have to clean, or work at, or mess with at all. Breathe consciously for a few seconds until you're feeling your breath move all the way from your toes to the top of your head.

Now put on a song that makes you relax. As the song starts to build, be aware of feeling your head sink into your pillow, feel your shoulders relax, your torso sink, your hips splay a little, your legs and feet let go. Continue to feel your breath moving through your body.

Use whichever hand is your nondominant hand. I write with my right hand, so I use my left hand for this exercise. Start behind your right ear, and barely touching your skin, make very soft, very, very slow circles or smiles. And again, listen to your body. Whichever one—the circles or the smiles—makes your body relax more is the motion to keep doing.

Slowly come down from behind your ear . . . feel that line all the way down, that little valley there? Very slowly . . . make circles or smiles down that valley.

When you get to your collarbone, you're going to do the same thing. Going all the way to the middle of your collarbone with circles and smiles.

Then work your way around your heart. Circles and smiles, going very softly. Gently thank your heart for taking care of you and your body. Continue doing circles, smiles, and add breathing and listening to the music. Whenever thoughts come in, make a smile on yourself and then a circle, and resume. Listen to the music. When you get to your belly button, make circles and smiles slowly down that center line . . . and then switch hands and start behind the opposite ear with circles and smiles. Dissolve any thoughts into the music and repeat the exercise on the opposite side of your body.

As you continue slowly making circles and smiles and breathing all the way through your body, you should feel your perineum—the area between your genitals and anus—expand. Breathe there, and then breathe all the way down your legs, out your feet, then back up through your inner and outer thighs, all the way up to the top of your head. Take your focus back to your heart. Spend some time there with this other hand. Notice how different it feels, if at all. Then down the middle channel to your belly button. Spend some time there, just giving it love. . . . Spend time on your stomach, your solar plexus, your pelvis, your rib cage, your sacral chakra, your lymph areas. Circling, smiling, whatever feels good.

VI

*When I was locked up
and they told me I was going
to lose my eye and potentially
become blind. I immediately got
a braille book and began to learn
braille. I don't give up, I fight.*

—WARREN HARRY

Your Starting 5

My sports-proficient friends cringe when I use sports analogies, but some are too good to pass up. A basketball coach has a full bench of players, but only five are chosen as the "starting five." They're team members who together create an unbeatable force or at least a force to be reckoned with. They alchemize into something that's bigger than the individuals.

A starting five isn't set in stone. Head coaches tinker with them to fit matchups. Teams trade players, and wholesale changes are common when a combination isn't playing well.

Putting someone in your starting five means you trust them deeply. I used to weigh my team by those I felt great around, but truly trusting someone is different from enjoying their company, admiring their ambition, or loving them. You can call someone a friend, but if you don't trust them enough to let them in when you need real help, then they aren't a starter. In the same way a professional athlete has a team of coaches, trainers, managers, and agents, or an actor uses a glam team to get ready for a scene or red carpet, we, as amateur adults, also need a team of people and friends to help us every single day in preparation for living. While the starters are commonly the best players on the team at their respective positions, each one knows that their spot on the starting five is earned—not assumed. That is why, in business, I advise my clients to go with shorter contracts with fewer options. This approach keeps everyone excited because the energy stays present for new opportunities.

This is the same approach I now take with my personal life. As we learn and grow, "deal memos" must be renegotiated with each new cycle of life. And I recommend that this be done with EVERYONE we are intimate with: family, partners, collaborators, neighbors, coworkers, etc. . . .

Curating Your Support Team

Build little YOU a community. If we believed ourselves invincible and certain in our uniqueness, we would know that competition, jealousy, and grasping are not needed. Take some time to think about your friends and make sure you are playing with a winning team, and I don't mean from a financially successful position. I mean analyze whether they fill you up and help you continually aim toward your highest potential.

Don't you think LeBron James or Michael Jordan labored over the right four players to be in their starting five? They knew the importance of picking the right teammates. So why do we not know that picking our Friends | Crew | Squad | Gang | whatever you call your ride-or-die is essential to ever possibly having a crack at winning the game of life? We tend to hold on to friendships out of habit, but your starting five—the people who are in your ear every day—need to be cultivated. No one is suggesting you casually discard friends over minor slights or squabbles. But you can give yourself permission to move on from certain people when the relationship no longer serves you, or to dial back their influence in your life. There's a difference between who starts the game and who comes in later. Friendships, like anything else, have seasons.

When was the last time your [friend, lover, mother, teacher, colleague, etc. . . .] supported you, and when was the last time you supported them?

If the answer is a long while ago or not at all, it might be time to reconsider that person's role in your life.

We all need a starting five in our lives. You know they have your back. You know you can count on them, and they can count on you. Together, you form a community that propels your success. Who are your starting five? If you don't have a team in place, create it. Cultivate it. Build it.

We have friends—but often we default to the same friendships (or the same kinds of people) throughout our lives. When was the last time you took a close look at your friends? Who grows you and improves you? Who asks you hard questions? Your starting five is the group around you that supports your growth, pushes you to live in your truth and your heart. This isn't about dismissing people you love; it's about creating a great group of people around you—a team—that gives you the support to win on the "rainbow level"—the fullest and highest expression of your humanity. That doesn't happen alone, and the people around you help to make it happen. Receiving help is not a failing. Your team can be made up of real people (ideally), or books or information or podcasts. In a perfect world, they are good friends, people who love us enough to help us in the daily act of living. These are the people who hold you up. Even the best—say, for example, an Olympic athlete—knows they can only win if they have a winning team. It isn't enough for them to be stellar at their specialty sport; the rest of the organization has to level up and they have to help them along. They cannot do it all by themselves—so why are you trying to do it all by yourself? The more we can stop being "crabs in a barrel," always competing with each other, and start to really understand that we are all brilliant beings with different information and magic to be shared, the more we share with each other, the more the glass ceilings start to break open. The more we support each other in growing our businesses, as well as in other areas of our lives, the less we will have a fever to find a partner who will fill that gap in our lives.

There was a time in history when we communed in circles together and healed, supported, elevated, and protected each other by sharing our collective stories. We passed down information; we explained how life, our bodies, relationships work.

Some laughed at our grandparents' walking groups and quilting circles, but they knew something about how important it was to connect with each other, to empower and entertain each other. Have we lost the impulse to collaborate?

A book club is a wonderful thing to participate in, but why not an investment club? A creative heartstorm–type think tank? An entrepreneurs' group or a tech meetup? Whatever it is, we need to create circles and find members to be a part of our starting five. Many male-leaning I know wouldn't think twice about going to all their friends and asking for $$$ to start or support their business, so why don't we all do that? Why don't we all feel entitled enough to ask for support or trust enough to freely give it?

Society has taught us that we can't trust each other or ourselves. I challenge you to go find humans who are really inspiring to you—some of them may not have overflowing abundance right now but are authentically I in a way that inspires you to do the same. Make them part of your circle to play a different position on your team. Maybe you see them once a month, maybe you have a phone call once a week, a conference call, a Zoom get-together. Maybe twice a year, you all meet at one destination, have a growth weekend or a challenge. Whatever it is, create a community that supports your growth. I'm not dismissing the importance of having hangout friends; we need to also have fun. But find | build the tribe that speaks in your native tongue and teach each other, share opportunities and information, and help each other rise.

Let's get our weight up.

TOOL

PICKING Your PARTNER

If you want a partner, a team member—one of your starting five or a circle of power—for love, expansion, career, or community, create a list of qualities you want in that person from the truth of your heart. Make the list very detailed. Feel into what this human is like and how you'd like to feel in this person's presence. And then . . . do not look for this person yet.

Embody the qualities on your list.

Once you've created a list, your job is to go through that list and become what you want to attract. Energy is magnetic.

Number one on my list is a partner/team member who believes in a connection to Spirit.

This partner/team member . . .

- has their own friends

- loves to be social with people that elevate their heart

- makes time to go inside, to hear themselves, to restore and grow

- loves life

- likes to try new things

- loves adventure

- loves to travel

- loves their family

- either has older children or doesn't want any

- respects all people and cultures, and doesn't look down on anyone

- respects all humans and learns from them

- is very comfortable in their skin and loves to explore intimately in all the ways

- is open-minded when it comes to food, art, and experiences

- loves me just as I am

- is not afraid to nudge me when they see me moving out of my vision

WHAT ELSE?

VII

Begin right this second,
loving and appreciating yourself
the way you do nature, art, kids,
and animals in your life. Not just
accepting but actually finding every
blemish, wrinkle, stretch mark,
gray hair, awkward conversation,
emotional overshare, and perceived
setback incredibly beautiful.
Beginning to believe that everything
is a tiny thread in the massive
unfinished masterpiece
of YOU!

Embodying the RAINBOW

Rainbows, similar to JOY, have gotten confused and misunderstood. And made to feel like a concept so much more shallow than what the true concept of a rainbow is.

And there have been many groups in history that have taken the concept of the rainbow as the perfect symbol or iconography or brand logo to comprise all the layers and all the complexities that represent them as an automatic *When you see this layer of colors, you get us*, from political groups to culturally defining groups that often want people to be experienced as more. It can't be in one color or one note or one scene or one strip of film. It's layered, it's complex, it needs the pre-quel.

Let's imagine a scenario in which there's a Group A and Group B, Group A being the ones who the system was built for and Group B being everybody else. And even in a group there are so many different experiences interwoven and inter-mingled with an opportunity to live in the luminosity of each color of that rainbow, of each shade of each color. In our sce-nario, Group A has been taught, encouraged, and raised to feel entitled to explore the full, vast expanse of each shade, its full offering, as the group learns what it needs as it leaves the boot-camp phase and enters the real game of life, diving deeper into the mission.

What I have found is that Group B in this scenario was not taught, was not allowed, to feel safe playing in, experimenting, and opening up to the wider I AM. Was raised clear in its love language of the safety of shared trauma rules for survival. Not entitled to stretch out, explore, and feel into the truth of our embodiment of our full rainbows.

There was this meme that was going around for a long time of this kid in water—it looked like they were in a vast ocean, terrified, feeling forced to learn to swim. And the well-meaning, loving adults around the child were obviously frustrated. You couldn't tell until the very end that the child was in water that was only up to its ankles. And finally, an adult pulled the child up to show the child that its deep fear, its huge emotions around the fear, was maybe not what it thought when it looked at it from a different angle, when it stood up to see really what it represented in terms of fear.

I could see that playing out in my own life, moving around through time, wanting nothing more than to be accepted and seen as a part of this giant group. With all the rules around an early positive experience for Group B, the first taste of emancipation, similar to a child learning to crawl. There's so much excitement and victory around that first crawl. It signifies the beginning of a new chapter, an opportunity for the baby, the child, to see the world from a different vantage point, to get closer to being able to move in all directions.

But consider if the child, once they learned to stand, hurt their hand or touched something sharp or had a reaction that was frightening to everything the child believed at the time. When they landed on the ground, that trying-to-stretch-out moment could have created an entire concept and language around the safety of staying in the crawl, staying on that level of all fours. Then it could have created religious philosophies to support the way to live at the crawl level, the essentials you need to learn to avoid horrible things happening to you when you feel and think you feel entitled to stand all the way up to the walk. To create entertainment and culture to remind everyone in Group B that it's essential to never get out of line, believing you can actually stand and walk, when so much went into how hard it was to even get to the crawl.

And now that we've figured out the way to live in a shared survival on the way to thrival in this crawl, we need you to understand that your mission is no longer the bigger mission, but how we no longer ever feel, any of us, the pain of stretching out beyond our crawl.

That may seem wildly dramatic, but just feel into the simplicity of that message, and then stand up and look around at this new truth. The truth is, the very reason I started writing this book began when I had a very young first child. I was on a local Brooklyn bus with my two-year-old daughter. A child sitting directly across from us caught our attention. They were having so much fun sitting backward in their chair, staring directly out at the whole world whizzing by. The child then turned to their caregiver and asked a question. At that point I am smiling from ear to ear at the confirmation I was getting as a new mother, watching a child stretch. To my surprise, the response to the child asking for more information was a literal violent shutdown. "Don't be nosy." And my heart broke into a thousand pieces. I was hurt for them. Those moments create our Avatars, to avoid fear. I realized right then, Oh, right, because it can be dangerous to live in a place that uses your second language, which you're still learning. Knowledge feels limited and thus everything seems unsafe. Or the two grandmas. The one grandma's bragging about their grandkids; the other grandma's downplaying their family's success: "Everyone's all right." Living from the tradition and a time when if we bragged on our kids they'd be _____ or raped or taken. It wasn't safe. All of those real experiences created the feeling of not enough, of a non-entitlement. We don't feel entitled. And yet a huge difference between Group A and Group B breaking glass ceilings and ascending beyond is thinking differently and believing we deserve it.

Getting back to my story about all of these messages in all these different situations, how to trip that little wire in the landmine of *This is not for you, Grace* was when I began to look into the bigger, overarching messages, propaganda. The whys of how we are supposed to live.

On that bus, I was holding my daughter's hand and could feel her whole body shudder. That collective trauma-pain moment. That night I couldn't sleep, so I wrote more than a hundred pages of how we kill the life out of people. My brain searched for the story to attach empathy. I made up a million stories, people who come to this country alone and | or under-resourced, not understanding the full language.

Just surviving, so you learn to keep a low profile. That might have been all she had access to, to explain all of that to them. I could feel in my own body the shutdown of life and then the beginning of the give-up. It felt like the slap heard around the world. It was the early '90s; sparing the rod, spoiling the child was still in full effect as a child-rearing concept. In those days, if you were in the street and any parent who knew you saw you misbehaving, they could spank you. Your teacher, neighbor, camp counselor had life permission to discipline you anywhere, in the name of raising good kids. Especially in cultures that had an understanding of the unwritten rules. That moment cemented for me that asking questions, leaning into more information, having a deep curiosity in our souls was not what was being taught to all this go-round on earth school.

I felt pressure to use a much firmer hand with my second child when he began acting out of control, which I now know is a deep crying-out for help and support: Help me figure out how to be my true self in a family that sees, believes, things are a very different way.

I lacked the awareness, tools, and most importantly support from my family to dive into alternatives. The same way we as a world are more patient and alter to support creatives versus academics and societally agreed-upon successful people. We are just beginning to understand individuality at its core and how every living being needs its own unique way of learning its path to the mission. And I can feel in my own life all the ways that I was metaphorically and literally slapped back down into my position, into my place in the world. To confirm for me how much harder it was to ask for more, how much more frightening it was. The ones who loved me found my questions threatening, and so I suppressed them out of fear of losing my place in my family, company, community, tribe, society.

I started writing this book, and it was called *Raising Powerful People . . . Starting with Yourself.*

If you come to a new place, how do you feel safe enough? Like the way some of us ask young people we know to help us with our phones, technology, or new words or cultural concepts. How do we learn to feel safe enough to let our collective children guide us to opening up to a new place and learning its ways, versus shutting down, guided by fear, and just wanting to survive life instead of leaning in to relearn how to thrive?

It's the concept of how you raise your children.

In a very general way, people who are supported by the system, I would say they give their children permission. We see that it's not mainly even a socioeconomic thing; it is an entitlement thing. No matter what you have in your pocket, there's a belief that you own a piece of this, whether it's this country, experience, the flag, just the way things are or whatever you're betting the farm on. And people, like the enslaved and Indigenous and immigrants who have not been supported by the system post–Founding Fathers. There is a concept baked in of *Lay low*. African-brought-to-America slaves, specifically, have an unspoken philosophy about appearance that I believe was created during emancipation. If you were a homeowner and you looked like a homeowner (oversimplifying but this is the concept), you were less likely to be arrested. That was important because being arrested meant the possibility of being put on a chain gang. Aka the beginning of corporate slavery.

Basically you were a _____, if you looked like you were a _____. But if you were a homeowner or proper citizen, then you were usually not messed with as much. To me, the effects of that are very obvious today.

When I was a preteen, I remember being with cousins on both sides of the world, from both systems, both groups. I had cousins who had brand-new sneakers that they were in love with. Looking at the sneakers made them happy, because they were a status symbol. They would carry a toothbrush because even a minor issue with the shoe had to be dealt with immediately. The aspiration was to not look poor and especially not look like you were on welfare or any government assistance. The goal was to at least look like you could afford to live and be received in the world as Group A.

I had other cousins who would get new shoes and find dirt and old them up on purpose, and quickly, so they didn't look rich. Didn't look like they were a part of Group A, not the lineage of Group A, and most importantly looked like they could hang with Group B.

I found that fascinating as a kid. I learned and leaned into each role until I got older and began to understand the social, societal, and systemic implications of both behaviors.

Systems built to enforce a literal and metaphorical robbing, erasing, and dismantling of a spirit's ability to illuminate. To criminalize and thus socialize a soul's belief that it cannot spread its own wings. A world, country, educational institution, religious | spiritual community, government, family, friend group, job, or partner who abuses their power over other humans creates a self-punishing humanity. Humans who can't even access enough worth in their own selves to reach or ask for more. There's very little entitlement, very little belief that you can ask for things.

The culture was built to make us self-govern our underserving behavior: *Don't talk* _____ or *We don't eat bougie food. That's not for you.* The beginning stages of that kind of boot camp was felt in that smack. We have a way of making sure we stay alive for survival but no concept of thriving, and so stay alive becomes a version of entitlement. It's what people hate and love about famous | rich people who question, buck, and stretch the systems. It's that deep entitlement to question that really gets the tongues wagging with judgment, which often is just envy. Or you could use your piece of the entitlement pie to decide to question nothing at all. Some believe that questioning, like that kid on the bus, could mean their life.

That piece has to change, and we can begin to chip away at it through our systemic inner change.

During the pandemic, I looked for ways to be helpful wherever I could and found a collective working for free to support humans in deep pain and overwhelmed with life. I worked virtually with many people one-on-one. I sat in on sessions involving other facilitators, social workers, religious leaders, life coaches, therapists, yogis, breath work instructors, mediation teachers, artists, moon circles, song circles, medicine healers, card nights. I give such a detailed list to highlight the many, many diverse help offerings I found, to give a true depiction of how the collective felt in the virtual world. I learned that the survival-of-the-fittest idea I grew up with was all about physical strength and life-out-in-the-wild abilities. The NEW survival of the fittest is all higher consciousnesses.

Some can't even access a way to communicate about what is actually coming and on many levels is already here. Back to the sneaker analogy. If we deem it impressive when we meet people who speak multiple languages, or even just their first language and then English so well, why do we take pride in isolating ourselves in one dialect that only communicates with humans who speak the same and thus by their very nature don't push each other to stretch out in any new directions? If the dream is success and evolving, then why do some believe that success is a vision cemented in our hearts during one period of our lives and then strive for that one concept of a dream, romanticizing its long-ago glory instead of opening up to trust the next dream in our hearts and all the new things that must be learned to achieve it?

I remember the first time I met a kid who was in private school on scholarship. We were both in middle school, but I went to a charter school that leaned toward a specialty in what we used to call English, which became social studies. They were telling me all about their new school, in a new neighborhood, with new friends, new social behavior, new pop culture references, language (if you take into account how different some preteens talk in different neighborhoods). I was so struck by what I was learning by listening to them that I could sense the way it felt in my stomach. In the '80s, kids that were so-called gifted and talented were often taken from their neighborhood school because it was shitty. And then put in a so-called better school. They won the big prize of having to learn everything in life over again to survive in their new habitat, AND they had to get exemplary grades, A+++.

Some dropped out of school and lost their academic scholarships, not because of their grades, but because they were on another planet with no connection to any of these things. So how can someone thrive in that way?

I am not at all crapping on the scholarship system. Thank

God for any gift of a gesture of equal lived experiences and the potential for settling so many core wounds. Ones that, if healed, would allow us as a world to set our unified sights on our world's much bigger issues. What I am pointing out is yet another way we build onto our Avatars and wonder why one day all of sudden we are emotionally, mentally, physically, and spiritually frozen.

The difference between Group A and Group B is FEAR!

Not venturing into unknowns.

Not safe.

Not certain.

Not taking no chances.

Group A believes they have the permission, feels entitled, to pioneer through life.

Entitlement

Belief in self

Connection to Source

Communing to hear, feel, fix, grow, and even ascend your inner system

IS THE NEW FITTEST.

Being out in the world alone so young, having to survive on my own resources, pioneering for a new way and foraging for sustenance on my journey toward entitlement. Learning to give myself permission to explore that full rainbow of offerings. And it's funny how our beliefs about certain symbols seem so set in stone, when for hundreds of years many symbols have changed their own meanings dramatically.

Whether we use the word rainbow or not, so many cultures have different ideology around that symbol. You could look at the wheels of the chakra, the way different seasons are described in photo and image and color, flags around the world. There's so much in how we express ourselves fully through the symbols of color and our connection to color in our own lives. The first Black American man who ran a nationwide campaign for president in the US, Jesse Jackson, used the word *rainbow* to describe his coalition. Many looking to be defined to the world as so much more than one thing identify with that iconography.

Imagine if we looked at nature that way, and we took the pieces that we felt were okay. Red, I don't know about red. Blue, hmm. So how do we feel about the sky and fire? What is our connection to ice and water? And do we not recognize these as soon as we see the color of them? Do we not understand what they are?

This is not an attack on anybody, or especially not blaming anybody. I feel up until now, in these previous chapters, it's clear that everyone is doing their best, operating with the knowledge they have right now, so there's no penalization in that. But if there are any feelings in your body, in your heart, in your psyche, or in your mind, at any moment that you'd like to stretch out a little wider, a quarter of an inch, toward your JOYous life, toward your big dream or even just feeling safe enough to wonder, this is the time to lean all the way into your life entitlement, your permission.

Your Yes

I've read a bunch of books in the last few years about saying yes or saying no. Reaching higher, aiming bigger. Every time I read one or went to a workshop, a seminar, or a retreat, I always felt so good while I was in the shared experience. And as soon as I was back out in the real world, the default world, the high started to get less and less as I realized I didn't understand how to access those things on my own. I understood every concept intellectually. I even understood a lot of the examples. I felt a lot of the experiences in the shared group settings or when reading their book and hearing the author's own life story blossoming from using the tools. But I couldn't get it. I couldn't access it in me. I couldn't make it a sustainable practice until I realized that there was a land mine of fears inside me, and I was not willing to trip any of those wires that I had been taught are crucial to avoid for my survival.

What were those wires? Oh, right. The belief that I even could, the permission in my soul to reach around some of these lessons, these oral traditions, religious concepts. Philosophical ways to live life that people who love me believed were imperative for my growth. A gift of their knowledge to make my life easier.

But boot-camping a future adult doesn't mean that you insert your own fears, your own pain, inside their energy bodies. It's re-raising ourselves alongside them. It's fact-checking our beliefs before we pass them on. It's making sure the JOY snacks are not expired.

If I don't know how to play volleyball, and I don't practice or prepare for a volleyball game, is it fair for me to play against a volleyball champion? Is there any way I can beat them if I don't know the language? We now live in an entrepreneurial spirit world. If you don't understand the language around the socialization of these communities, you don't have a chance.

I am making cards with consciousness, ascension words, expressions, and slang. Funny popular-culture images will teach the simplest meaning of the new concept. A cheat code, if you will, mostly for myself, like flash cards, and to translate to my starting five. The new language needs games, and humans need fun, so let's gamify learning; let's get as excited about growing as we do sports on the screen. Life school—the levels never end.

Those are the wires we're trying to trip, right there.

I want to be a bajillionaire, an influencer, have _____, _____.
I want to change the world.

I want all these things. . . .

What's in the way of those desires?

The firewall is the stories you have adopted that are anti to the voice trying to get through to you that believes that you deserve it, that you can even reach entitlement.

Which is why I was saying when I went to these workshops and all these things, I was getting the message; intellectually I was feeling into what they were saying. But when I went back out into the world, it did not feel safe for me to operate in. That right there is the thing. So how do we get to that? That's what I want to talk about right there.

Entitlement is loaded with the beginner's mind and an openness to the JOY of our heart in its truth. Our belly feeling relaxed, breathing fully in our bodies, having all systems firing at once so that we have our whole team engaged. I am absolutely not against Christianity or any religious | spiritual philosophy that promotes and supports TRUST, LOVE, FAITH, GRACE, and JOY. It's an overall bigger point. But it needs to be untangled so each group can hear it in a respectful way. I am highlighting questions for us all to ask ourselves. Can we feel into our truth in connection to the businesses built to keep us tethered to messages that make us small and pressure us to make beliefs outside of ourselves into gospel? Keep us separate from spirit and use a mediator to communicate with our individual version of God? What we must understand is that those small things tear away at the fabric of entitlement and belief that we deserve. Lack of entitlement, aka there's a way we have to behave. Trauma being a group's only singular connection point allows for cancel culture and Twitter to govern and regulate us into staying in our collective lane(s).

I was a creative director for thirty-plus years in the music industry. I worked with many amazing artists and always encouraged them to see how much further they could go. I would say, "You have to have an authentic connection with your fans for them to feel you.

"Connecting people to their gifts—which live in the heart—is going to produce success. When we are connected to our gifts through our hearts, we are illuminated from the inside, and we are strong. Instead of wanting to hold on to what is mine, we're open and available to share our Rainbow Light."

I felt growing up that I was a mishmash of traditions and backgrounds that often made me feel confused and out of place.

Fitting in, assimilating, not standing out, code switching was what I was taught to do to survive. Never feeling connected to others, to any particular culture, religion, or tradition, or to myself was an empty and confusing existence. Similar to anyone living a lie. Eventually, I evolved to accept that I was going to be a rainbow—that one identity didn't have to define my entire self.

You can create your own rainbow life—a life that expresses the different colors of who you are. A rainbow means you express yourself in all your dimensions. We are the collection of things that fill up our hearts—all the things we enjoy and appreciate. How do we live fully expressed as who we are?

Play Hard and Let Down Your Guard

As we grow up, we get better at masking ourselves, creating representatives that we send out to interact with everyone in our world. We try on different behaviors to figure out what works in manipulating whatever response we want from various people. As babies, we smile and laugh to drum up food or attention; as adults, we reconfigure ourselves to perform according to society's bizarre standards or to get our desires satisfied—to feel wanted, loved, appreciated, and | or valued. Therefore, we are never in honest and vulnerable exchanges with anyone. We are managing everyone else's expectations and feelings but our own. But when we create moments of JOY every day, we clear the air of everyone else's expectations. We block out all the noise with the rhythm of our own beating heart. And it's in these moments that we forget about the rules and tune in to the path we really want to take.

In terms of my own path, throughout my career in entertainment, I helped the best in class get deeply connected to their authentic voice, working in tandem with hundreds of artists to unearth their musical gifts. When I embarked on my own journey, it became clear to me that the answers we need exist inside each of us. The trick was figuring out how to find them and how to tune out the naysaying voices.

I dropped out of school in tenth grade to work full-time, to pay rent + the grown-people bills piling up around me. One of the voices I had to learn to silence over the years was the one that worried about how little I know and how little education I've had. I lived daily in deep fear of making mistakes, all that I might do wrong. Through play, I came to understand that nothing we do is ever really wrong. We learn from every step we take. It took a long time to get here, but I'm proud I arrived, at least in seeing the full thread.

You've got a unique gift, too. It's easier to work with it once you recognize what it is.

Working with so many celebrated artists over the years made it clear to me that we are all creators in different ways, and tapping into JOY cracks open our hearts to reveal the brilliance of our own guiding light. It became obvious that JOY was more than just fun—more than a half hour of sillies. In fact, JOY is a key step in reaching our highest potential. Thus began the practical application of the Revolution of JOY. Now, through group events and one-on-one playdates, I work with an incredibly diverse assortment of clients in tapping into the birthright of JOY that ultimately illuminates their destined path. And the best part is that once your path is lit, you can light the way for others.

Be the Light!

I'm not telling you anything you haven't heard before, but if you want a great life, you have to get out of your own way. You have to stop acting like someone's gonna save you, like somebody has a magic answer. It's actually in you. Happiness is a choice, manifesting your great career is a choice, being in a great partnership is a choice. But it literally starts from understanding that you know the answers. You have to actually be honest with yourself about them and start to do the real work of applying them to your life.

I was at a dinner with a friend I was helping with the marketing of their film. In other words, this was a work dinner. Out of the blue, one of the women from the PR firm asked me to help her with a really personal issue. I've trained myself to not give unsolicited advice to others, as even that is a judgment of where they are and what I believe is needed. Clear boundaries keep spiritual egoism in balance for me.

Though this dinner was not the ideal setting for this kind of deep and potentially exposing conversation, I had to acknowledge to myself that this was clearly an opportunity to share, directly from Spirit. She said, "I'm terminally single, and I don't understand why."

I said, "The first thing is . . . this idea we have that we have to look for a partner is false. Whenever you're looking for something outside of yourself, you're missing something in your own life. Let's start with how you go about filling yourself up. Humans attract humans who mirror each other. If you're looking for something to make you feel better about yourself— in other words, coming from lack—that's what you will attract. Another human who feels inadequate, who will be looking to you for validation. When they don't get from you what they think they are missing, they will leave. The hack or cheat code of Love is to feel into your heart how you want to feel in communion with your lover. What do they bring as expansion to the union? Then, do they work to vibrate as that full list? I would ask you to look at your own life for things that you could throw yourself into—things, projects, exercises, creative ventures—that make you excited about your own life. Projects give you so much JOY that you literally become a magnet for all kinds of energies (options) to drop in to and mirror for you what you are generating in your own soul."

I studied her for a moment and then asked if I could share an insight. "YES, please" was the response.

"I feel it's been a long time since anything's been happening down there," I said.

She giggled self-consciously and said, "Yes . . . you're right. . . . It's been four years since I've had any form of sex."

I replied, "I'm not even talking about partner sex. Do you ever touch yourself? We are animals, we smell each other. . . . We forget that about ourselves. If you're not even giving yourself pleasure, if you're not filling yourself up, you're not lighting up all the full panel in your own body. I recommend that you create a nightly juicy-with-yourself ritual. . . .

"Light some candles, wear something that turns you on, put on some music, and explore your own body. Light yourself up, and then you'll be so full of JOY and excitement that you'll see . . . you'll attract everything. You're gonna have to start running from people. Hehe!

"Go back to the childlike qualities that made you feel alive and excited as a kid. Remember when you used to dance so much that you would fall down exhausted, when you swam so much that when you went to sleep you still felt yourself swimming, when you went to an amusement park and you went on so many rides that you were dizzy for hours? As one of my teachers says, 'When you are living inside JOY, not just enjoying, you will literally attract other people with that same vibration.' Then you will be setting your life up to be in a place where you're always doing what you love. . . .

"What do you love?" I asked her.

She said, "I love to ride horses."

I said, "When's the last time you rode a horse?"

"When I was a kid."

"I hope that next time I see you," I said, "you'll tell me that you've found a stable, have a horse, and that you're riding. Because when you are in flow with your own heart's desires . . . that's when you as your partner will show up."

Anyone, everyone else, will have to bring even more JOY than you supply yourself.

You Are Your Own North Star

When I say that play lights up your North Star and activates your internal GPS, what I'm really saying is that JOY frees you up to listen to your gut—your inner guide.

The more I played and practiced at JOY, the more I realized how all these bizarre societal beliefs—all these shoulds and shouldn'ts—had been getting in my way. They were so loud, I forgot I even had an inner guide.

Think about it this way: The brain is where we worry about shit—money, looks, pleasing people—and all those worries get so loud that they distract us from the things we care about, what we actually want and what inspires us.

On the other hand, JOY is spontaneous; it comes to you without thinking. JOY is listening to the heart—which is entirely your own, while the brain is mostly filled with information other people have put into it. When you're experiencing JOY, the heart takes over, it glows. When you're acting from the heart, you silence all the brain blah, blahs, and you can suddenly hear your own gut. You can listen to it. And you know what? You make better choices, choices driven by your truth—not society's, not your friends', not by the shoulds and shouldn'ts and can'ts that have gotten way too comfortable living in your brain like houseguests who just won't leave.

When you're in your head, you're dead. You're comparing and despairing. But when you're driven by your own JOY, you're in touch with your truth. It's like all the many mechanisms of your internal compass are suddenly finely tuned.

TOOL

CREATING with JOY

Nothing kills the ego like playfulness, like laughter. When you start taking life as fun, the ego has to die; it cannot exist in its current form anymore.

Has it been a loooong time since you laughed so hard your cheeks hurt? Then you have moved too far away from your pre-Avatar state. The untethered levity of the space before all the judgment and pressure of other people's rules and expectations. Our adult lives are packed with working and family commitments. We don't make feeling great and having pure fun our top priority.

When did we stop playing?

When did we give up on even trying to take a step toward living to our full capacity?

The true love of self resides in the release of control and the pleasure of your laughter. This transformative playdate of art, music, dance, games, and full-on play will start to dispel the myth that pleasure is a luxury and not THE tool of transformation to achieve your daily state of JOY. Chisel away the cement of fear formed around your heart and crack yourself open to _____.

Be creative for thirty minutes a day without being attached to what the final product looks like. Throw your perfectionism out the window and create simply for the sake of creativity and play. Draw, write, dance, garden, paint, sculpt, sing, or come up with something you like to do, even if you don't think you do it well. If there is a finished product, do not share it with anyone but yourself.

VIII

In your life there's peaks and valleys and sometimes we regress, and we don't even know we regress. You just have to learn how to accept all of your mistakes and learn to love yourself again.

—MARY J. BLIGE
ELLE MAGAZINE

Who Owns LOVE?

I am polyamorous when it comes to religion and spirituality. If every metaphysical teacher on the planet throughout millennia is teaching some version of It all boils down to LOVE, then how can anyone own it?

Or believe that their particular brand of religion, spiritual philosophy, etc. is the superior one that you should build your entire life on?

How can anyone decide they would kill for love?

How can we truly love our neighbors if the idea is marketed to us that we can kill them if it is in defense of whatever version of _____ we are trained is the actual one?

We have been marketed to about love—language and ideas that turn love into a weapon. How can you be expansive and open if you are bombarded by propaganda that sells a false message about love? Look at all the "love messaging" around YOU, and understand the ways it corrodes what actual love is and how it affects you personally.

The Noise of Love vs. The JOY of Love

I've spent my fair share of time thinking about where my marriages went wrong—and how to avoid such ill-fated romances in the future. Guess what? The same way that the noise and naysayers of the world (the Shouldn't-Should-Can't Crew) drown out JOY and confuse our understanding of what we want out of life—they're also really good at warping your love life.

When we first come into the world, everyone around us is equally beguiling: They're all love. But we quickly learn to focus on the person most necessary to our growth and survival (Mom, Dad, caretaker, etc.). If baby talk gets us a bonus feeding, then baby talk it is! At an early age, we understand that we have to conform to certain expectations simply to ensure that we can get what we need.

This is how we first learn to be people pleasers—and we bring these subconscious survival tactics wherever we go. Even to romance.

Especially to romance.

When it comes to love, we're all sold a whole bunch of propaganda—that love heals you, that love saves you, that love marks the ultimate moment, the end of the story, roll the credits.

Love that comes from the outside is never entirely true, because we perform to keep it coming. It's the natural evolution of our first survival skill. Or it's silencing your anger, curbing your desire, smothering your truth, turning a blind eye. We're willing to do whatever it takes to feel like our love story has its happily-ever-after firmly in place. We start performing, squelching JOY and our truest desires. When our gut tells us that something isn't right, we ignore it—because the stakes are too high to risk the love story we're so desperate to have. We stop expecting JOY; we suppress our wants and then we lose track of them completely. We ignore our gut for so long, we forget it's good for anything but ice cream.

I love love that comes from the inside.

That's the stuff.

We're sold the idea that being a good life partner is a particular set of things—but over time all it means is: Just be nice. Just be quiet. Just avoid confrontation. Suck it up and do without the drama.

Just ignore your feelings, your gut, your essential inner truth. Just keep quiet and live your life | lie.

One weekend I was with my niece and she blew me a kiss clear across the park. I smiled and my heart sang and melted at the same time.

But by the fourth time I watched her do it, I understood that this kiss-blowing was becoming a thing. She does it all the time because she knows she'll get a warm reaction. Nothing wrong with that in theory, but overindexed or in-replacement-of-her-own-nourishing love becomes a searching-for-love habit.

"We've got to watch out for reinforcing that kiss-blowing move." I very gently held out the thought for my sister's reaction (not wanting to give unsolicited advice that is received as a forced gift). "Before she decides that being cute and sweet is THE way to get love."

All I want for her, for myself, and for YOU is to embody love and keep it by staying true to our own heart.

All of us live in different degrees of performative love. Always worrying what other people think, worrying if we're liked, and we adjust ourselves to be accepted. Every time we do that, we make ourselves smaller. Making sure everyone is happy means losing track of our truest selves. But when you practice JOY, your heart manages to wrestle all the control away from your head, you silence the world of external expectations, you light up your inner North Star, and as it guides you, you're able to trust your gut. All this is to say you end up making decisions you can trust. This applies to figuring out what you want to do with your life—and it also helps you discover the best people to have by your side, your starting five. At that point, it's safe to let love be your intention, your purpose, and your point.

Lost and Found

I personally learn and grow through experience; I dive deep when I feel heart-connected with someone. That could be in any way: creative collaboration, intimate lovers, family, best friends, adventurers, co-yoga-ers, people I dance with, people I like to have adventures with, roommates. As soon as we start to get vulnerable, it feels good. Heart's like, *Let's go!* And we're there and we're going, and we're starting to say crazy stuff that we can't believe we're saying out loud. What am I doing? I can't say that. One of my beloveds calls it diarrhea mouth, which is gross. But it is; it's coming out and you can't even clench your butt cheeks enough. Your mouth is betraying you. But it's because it feels safe and it wants to; that's what it's here to do. You connect, you grow, you connect, you grow, you share, you learn new things, you inspire each other.

Now you feel exposed; you're those naked winter trees again. Then, all of a sudden, Ego and Brain try to shut it down. What are you doing? They are running down some hall (I visualize Ego | Brain racing around backstage, trying to find Heart before the message is blasted from the main stage). Trying to get to you fast to pull the plug, or turn the system off, or cover your mouth, or do something, because you're about to kill the whole situation. You're about to bring the show down. That's when we start to move past our boundaries, we begin looking for something forever and never feeling complete because that's not even how we're wired. What we do need is that buzzword *self-love*; that's what that is. You start treating yourself like your own client. You start doing the things you do for yourself that you do for lovers you want to impress. Do the same things you do for your children, parents that you take care of, the boss who's overdemanding. Start to make sure that you give yourself if not more, at least the same amount. Then you know what happens? Let there be space in your togetherness. I say it this way: You have to be your singular self in every relationship.

Another incredible human I love wrote in their book that they wanted to be for their child their full self all the time. They want the child to know how big and amazing they can be in the world, and for that self to never get tainted, robbed, diminished in any way.

They wanted to show their child that it's a wonderful thing to love what you do and love. To enjoy being with your friends and being in partnership. To have a project sometimes that enriches you, that you're on fire about, and balance that with inner exploration. Mirroring for them a full human.

On the plane they say to put your own oxygen mask on first. If you hold on to that feeling, then you're always in your heart, and your heart only wants to love. Instead of attacking others, getting defensive, living in victim consciousness, holding on tighter, wanting to control another's every movement, or being upset that they have other friends. Many people believe that unconditional love is the way to be in love, but real love has conditions.

Real love has many boundaries, which is the foundation and | or container for honesty in love. It is safe to be ourselves. When we feel unsafe, we morph into somebody else, which I have done over and over in relationships. I am a super senior on the lesson of love. That's why I really feel so excited to share these jewels because on the other side of that is just true relationships where everyone is held. They get to brag; they get to be honest. We get to be our full, vulnerable selves, trusting life with the safety that no one's judging us.

Then you never have the conversations about how you've changed. There's a lot of things we do, and part of it is not our fault because for years and years there was a concept that some of us couldn't have opportunities if we weren't bought by the other one, if we weren't owned by the other one in some way, and so we started having to make up a lot of falseness for the business of marriage. What does it mean, and how do we show up for it, and how we get it and how we land it? Just like a job. Some people campaign for these things because they feel like they have to lock it down, that it's a part of succeeding; they're locking themselves in a soul prison. Then they grow and morph, and people fall out of love because they don't recognize the person they fell in love with in the first place. They went to every lost-and-found booth they could find. Some people seek counsel from their religious leaders, therapists, their family that supports them. They have affairs, they abuse, they rage. They become addicted to other things, looking for the sweetness in life, looking for pleasure, because they're not getting it in their home, in the place they dwell, because they've locked themselves in with someone who can't see them.

Find yourself. Represent them to yourself.

Be very tender. Treat this little self like you just had a baby. Whatever kind of baby, a business of a baby, a human baby, a whatever. You have this precious thing; it's a giant crystal, a trophy of the greatest honor that you could ever have as an athlete, whatever floats your boat. But when we live in understanding that we're the chief energy officers of our own lives, we know that feeling amazing, illuminated, feeling deep JOY in our hearts, freely trusting life, is possible. We, as we are, are the embodiment of a gift to everyone around us, because what is good for you when you're being honest with your soul, and integrity, and wanting what's best for everyone's highest potential, then what you want is good for the whole, even if you can't see how that journey all the way unfolds.

Fearless Love

In the middle of a divorce, I was meditating and had an epiphany about how I arrived at the place that I currently am. I realized that I had this desperate need to not be like my mother. This desperate need to be married, to prove that I could be in a partnership and to prove that I could "have it all."

I started to think about having it all and what that means. Can you really have it all? Can you be the chairhuman, be the tech, and also a good salesperson at the same time? Would that person have all of the same qualities at the same time? I realized then that we as humans have been sold a bill of goods. We've been set up to fail. Women specifically are reminded every day how unpowerful we are and that we need to achieve the American Dream (which is to be married, with two children, by the age of thirty-five, in a beautiful home and with an incredible career outside of the family—not to mention being fabulous in bed with the best boobs and ass imaginable). That dream is not realistic, and in my experience, no one can achieve that. What are we teaching our young? We are showing them that they are wrong. We teach kids to be fearful, to be afraid. The saddest thing of all is that we teach children to not love themselves, through the mirroring of our actions. Others are taught that same lesson as something to overcome. Some are already taught to understand setbacks. I read this book and the writer relates the story of how the women in her family know exactly how to deal with men. The women in her family all have successful marriages, because they carry this information. The book basically breaks down the idea that men are different, and if you want to be in a happy marriage, you need to treat them differently.

Ughhhhh. For example, men have transition times when they walk in the door, so don't talk to them right away, and only talk to them during hearing times. My reaction to that book was simple: Where the fuck is our book? Where is the book that tells the whole planet to jump through hoops for female-defining people? We as women like to talk through things relentlessly and to process feelings multiple times. We need a book that teaches men how to treat women in order to live their best lives.

I believe we desperately needed to start seeing more powerful versions of ourselves on-screen. We come from tribes of strong women, warriors, witches, sorcerers, and Goddesses. Taught to be geniuses, to harness their light. Today's culture teaches women to have beautiful bodies, to be great wives. I'm not diminishing being married. Marriage is extremely important, but its importance is not seen in the way it is intended. It's two businesses coming together. Creating bigger empires. With the industrial revolution and the advent of science and industry, marriage changed. Men now had the ability to choose their path; they no longer had to marry into someone's family. As a result, there's an entire generation of men who left wives who weren't multifaceted. These scorned women then taught the next generation to lean into succeeding as the goal, creating a lopsided, unbalanced concept of living.

I read another book about how you live in the gender role that you choose to be in the partnership that you actually want. If you always take the lead in relationships, then that's okay! If you're okay with your significant other not earning as much, or being a stay-at-home parent, then that's something that you're choosing. But if you want to be cherished, then you have to sign up for a partnership with someone who will take the lead. Therefore, you can sit back, receive, and be cherished. The most important part of the book is understanding that there are times in your relationship that will shift. There will be times to receive and times to lead. It's not to surrender or to know one's place, it's admitting that it's okay sometimes to let someone take the reins.

A thriving relationship, designed for the highest of all involved, has each being both the Orchid and the Gardener, when needed.

I have a pack of friends who are amazing and aggressive toward life. I've started this exercise where when I'm around any of them, I allow them to take over. It began about five years ago, when I was on a trip with six of my friends. We were all fighting to have our voice heard and our plans made. But I realized that in my love for them, it was nice to let them lead. That has taught me that being a participant and not a leader doesn't take away from my strength. It actually is a strength, because I get to sit back and enjoy the ride, I get to trust and experience, which allows me to actually breathe. It gives my brain and my heart the permission to just InJOY. When you're taking, you're not learning. When you're talking, you're not receiving or hearing. When people ask, *Who needs therapy?* the answer is anyone who was born to parents. We're humans raising humans. We are going to make mistakes. But if we can look at each other and learn from our communities, we then find value in everything.

TOOL

ESTABLISHING Healthy BOUNDARIES

Build a Negative Space Calendar. Actually block out time on your calendar for you. Make it as sacred and immovable as a doctor's appointment. Put in a location, turn off your phone, and make a plan for how you want to spend ME time. Do not use it to do household chores, or to slide into work. This is time for Y-O-U. Support and love yourself by connecting to how you want to feel at all times. And then begin to define your boundaries by thinking about how many hours/mins/secs per day/week you truly want/have energy to spend with others.

Once you sense what FEELS the best in YOUR body, make your negative space calendar. Slot in how many minutes/hours you need every day just for you. Do you NEED/WANT to dance, play, create, rest, hang with lovers/friends/family? Then make those the priority.

IX

When there is no enemy within, the enemies outside can't hurt you.

—AFRICAN PROVERB

Raising Powerful People . . . Starting with ME

How do I want to live?

How do I want to feel?

What career do I want?

A friend identified how much time I spent caring about other people and their opinions of me. I had to re-parent myself—and that's when I discovered that pleasure and JOY are more of a truth serum for living our lives. We focus on pain, panic, and difficulty—and how to overcome those. But if we train our eyes to stay at the horizon of JOY and raise ourselves up there, we go back to square one—re-parenting ourselves. If I'm messed up because I didn't get a fair shake with parenting—if the plant was planted wrong—then I have to go back and redo the soil, the seeds, and the fertilizer.

We spend so much time judging ourselves for what is not beautiful about ourselves. We judge our bodies, our actions, our lack of success, how we interact with people, what we said that wasn't right, or what we didn't say when we needed to. If we spent even half that amount of sadly wasted time loving the shit out of ourselves, the way we do nature, art, kids, or the animals in our lives, who knows what our lives would look and feel like? Not just accepting but actually finding every blemish, wrinkle, stretch mark, gray hair, awkward conversation, emotional overshare, perceived setback incredibly beautiful. Overwhelmed by the seemingly insurmountable problems of the world and lack of belief that I alone can effect change, we do nothing. Being a bright light in the world is a revolutionary act of leadership. If we all felt immense JOY and security from our love being rooted within, we would unite, support each other, and see each other as unique gifts. We would be luminous. We would be a revolution of JOY.

The Grace Tour

There was a year in my early fifties when I realized I had yet to learn how to live in the complete balance of trust, faith, and self-love. When you actually surrender and truly live in faith, you are 1,000 percent on the ride, using tools, leaning into your starting five and your other resources to support yourself and continue to activate the courage of your heart to expand in every direction and color. You are not preplanning, controlling, future-ing, or past-ing. You are living in a state of equanimity, meaning that you understand that every step, every situation, every piece of the journey IS the journey. Going on the adventure of self-discovery feels scary because you never have the comfort of certainty. You're walking down a very long hallway without being able to see the door at the end that will open to the next adventure or opportunity. You simply must have complete faith that you will find it there. When your eyes are shining with excitement and the anticipation of new opportunity, and your heart is open and trusting, you're connected, completely strapped into the ride, ready to face the new, the change, the growth. Whether I judge the ride to feel good or not to feel good, or to be fun or not fun, to be comfortable or uncomfortable, it's all part of IT.

It's the super-low peaks and surprisingly high valleys. It's ME. Instead of guessing what the movie is in the first few minutes, it's allowing myself to be taken on the journey of the artist, the director, the writer, the person I'm in conversation with, my own self to finish something. I'm InJOYing every piece of it. Instead of ripping the wrapping paper off the present, I'm noticing first the beautiful detail, the full offering. The whole experience starts from the excitement of receiving, of knowing that there's something in there just for you.

This is now my life practice.

It's loving that, feeling safe in it, being completely present in it, which is just not being in my head, opening my heart to feel it, to see it, to hear it, to experience it, to taste its energy, to feel its vibration. And move on to the next second and do the same thing; rinse and repeat. So, it was very amusing to see a giant pattern come together for me that I didn't even know was another place that needed an upgrade, that needed me to breathe into the big jump into whatever is unfolding right now.

I had a really complicated year. . . . It was one where I was in the most dysfunctional codependence that I've ever experienced but also the greatest high of excitement, and new opportunities, and the layers of my onion just sliding off and opening up to even more spicy juiciness that, yes, sometimes will make you cry, but also will make everything else delicious when you figure out how to receive its medicine, and its love, and its offering. I also was in such a beautiful space of starting to really see myself, to understand my own gift and my own gift to myself, and my true mission on this planet. Those things were starting to be in a direct, sometimes violent, war with each other. I was already broken up. It had happened a couple weeks prior to this NYE trip. But in true Grace fashion, I did not want to upset everyone around us who had been invited. I wasn't ready to speak outside myself about what was going on with anyone yet, as it was important to me to get off the ride and really figure out how and why and when this was going to be revealed.

The core belief of that was when it was best for the whole family, when it was going to be the least amount of damage. I planned the last day before the new year to be a healing day. One healer's gift was reading palms. So, this palm reader spoke to me, with a beet-red face of embarrassment. She looked at my hands, studying them each for a long time. She finally looked up, met my eyes with a searching glare, and said . . .

"It says you should—I can't believe I'm saying this—do drugs and masturbate. I am so sorry; I have never heard that come through before."

I thought it was so amusing. One, because she was so freaked out by even having to say any of that. It was funny how much I thought of myself as this very free and open-minded person. But at the time I still was kind of hiding from Spirit whenever I touched my body anywhere near the zones that I'd been told my whole life were dirty, or to be hidden, or only for one use, or all the very strict rules around one particular body part versus another. And so I enjoyed that in a wanting-to-share way and that not pulling it in internally is a big piece of a puzzle on my path, on the scavenger hunt of life. It seemed complicated for some reason that I didn't understand.

Cut to many years later . . .

As is obvious, I LOVE to read, so, I read an interesting book that explains the concept of what it really means to live in faith and presence. It is moving with each giant YES as a direct order from LOVE itself. Humans I adore have been on me to come visit them in a region of the world that my brain deemed an H-E-double-hockey-sticks. I didn't realize that the fear was just a way to not take the steps further on my path, me sabotaging the end of this book, understanding that closure opens a door for so much more. That's such a new concept of GRACE in all ways. Of course, when I finally let my HEART lead the way and finally touched down, all of ME lit up like a football field of disco balls. I was literally holding the door shut with both hands, while the open door I was praying for was flying and flinging open in all directions. I was meditating on and looking for signs about where to continue to blossom. Where in the world would I find the people that effortlessly light me up as much as I enjoy lighting up others? As I went to the place that was on the absolutely no list, the absolutely not-an-option list, I was all of a sudden dropped into a feeling that I honestly hadn't experienced since my teenage years, or at least early twenties, of being in universal flow. I felt like a kid again in the ways that matter. I was writing, creating art, playing in the way I InJOY playing, out in the water, canoeing, paddleboarding, bike riding, hiking, doing yoga, dancing, and having expansive conversations.

Fifty times in one conversation: "What does that mean? Tell me more," which is my absolute favorite thing.

I was home.

When I take my hands off the wheel, my life really is a self-driving vehicle in that it's just pulling from the information and data in my own heart of my true wants. Which is why I'm learning to keep them clear and pure. It guides me beyond my wildest dreams to the expansion of those dreams. The one I didn't even know if I could have even accessed because they were beyond what I'd already sourced and already seen and experienced in my life thus far. Every time I land in a new peak or valley, I'm humbled by its bigger-than-my-imagination gift, or at least the one I allow myself to see and tap into at this point. As I drifted off to sleep, I realized that I hadn't actually put that work in that I was promoting, which is being your actual best lover, touching yourself the way you touch your lover. I mean, if I treated myself the way I treated brilliant, creative, artistic people that I've been very intimate with, there's a constant curiosity, an excitement for everything that they have to share, a real coveting and enjoying every bit of their entanglement, and the collaboration of our most vulnerable selves.

There's so much patience, and love, and excitement, and support for the ideas and the conversations and the things. If I really slowed everything down that I do around and to myself, the way I touch myself, the way I look into my own eyes, like I would to an incredible lover. When I did that, ideas and ideas and ideas poured in, which is always my reward for good behavior, a sign and signal that I'm walking softly in the direction of the actual path.

Would You Date You?

If you're looking for a partner, someone you potentially want to spend, at the very least, a good portion of your life with, why would you be looking for them in places you don't enjoy?

I decided I was ready to date. I'd never really dated in my life. It was just not how it'd gone down. But it seemed like a whole new fascinating foray. I was especially interested in understanding where people were at, because people are fascinating to me. It felt like an opportunity to do some intimate investigative reporting. *Would you date you?*

However, I had to sit down and really think about what I wanted: *If I'm going to be in a life with someone who is my "ideal partner," or part of my intimacy team or a great lover, whatever it ends up being, don't I have to feel into what I would want that experience to be? And then from that feeling of what I want my day-to-day to be like, how I want to be supported? How much time I need for myself? And how much time I want to donate and dedicate to a relationship? What I want it to be about? What the mission statement is?*

I was hanging out with a group of friends—all different ages and all different expressions of human—discussing dating, relationships, and who we would want as an ideal partner. We ended up writing these fantastical lists of all the characteristics we wanted in a prospective partner.

How many of those items on your list do you actually embody right now? And would you date yourself?

This is really the simplest point of all this. Would you, if you were put in front of you as a choice, date yourself? Answer really honestly. Really look at yourself. . . . This is not a judgment thing. This is not *Would you date yourself because you're horrible*. No, I'm saying, just be honest about this process. If you're looking for a new job and you see that it says oncologist and you have no actual training for that, what is the likelihood that you're going to get that position?

And this is the same with everything, right? Everything is everything. One of my big things was that I wanted a partner who had a daily yoga and meditation practice, but I didn't really have a dedicated daily practice. . . . I had one when it worked for my schedule, when I wasn't too tired, when it was convenient, when it looked good for The Gram, but not a real dedicated practice, because it just felt good in my being and was part of who I was, which is what I was expecting of every partner. I had to admit to myself that loving someone and enjoying what they bring to the table might be different, but equally perspective shifting. So, this is where we start. Would you date you?

TOOL

Apply LOVE to Places Inside That HURT

I'm not going to lie, some of the moments in my life—my divorces, with their heartbreaks and feelings of failure—were crazy painful, but they were instructive. To tell the truth, until I had those experiences, I hadn't known that I could feel such deep pain. Before my divorces, there was always someone else around and I'd turn my focus to them or I'd throw on a mask, as we're all taught to do when we're young. "I'm fine. I'm fine. No, it doesn't matter. It's all good." When you find yourself in pain, practice speaking sweetly and soothingly to yourself. "My Love, why don't you let me put you in a bubble bath?" If you feel, as I did, stuck in this area of your life, begin a genuine courtship with yourself. Be gentle, take it sloooow with yourself. Remind yourself to recognize that you're safe, amazing, loved beyond words, and that You Got This. The next time you pass a mirror . . . STOP, SMILE AT YOURSELF, LOOK DEEPLY INTO YOUR OWN EYES and say . . . "I Love YOU, _____."

Through this process, you let yourself love yourself, and you find that true love comes through you, not just to you.

TOOL

I Have _____

When I get really freaked out about something, the loop in my head goes, *No one's here for me. No one's going to help me, blah, blah, blah, blah, blah, blah, blah.* And then I go into that *I can't do anything, and it's never going to work.*

I start making it a very big trauma response instead of saying to myself, "I've got this." This is not about material things at all. It's about the things in yourself that you're proud of. Different than the I AM, which are the things you are. This is about acknowledging the qualities you've cultivated within yourself. One of the things on my list is I have a lot of love to give, but again, that starts with me, so what do I have? And it took me a long time to cultivate that, so that's not a caretaking thing. That's understanding that love is my superpower and I have a lot of love to give to myself first. I have healing energy. That's part of my magic, my voice, my touch, and what I say. I have great ideas. I have a beautiful smile, a young spirit. I have a great attitude. I am proud of my connection to Spirit, my sense of humor, and those are all the things I have because I worked at them, and I cultivated them and realized that they were jewels.

X

The next time you catch yourself "should-ing" on someone, stop and ask yourself if that advice is actually for YOU.

Creating a New Paradigm!

M ost of what I believe and know and have bet the farm on, bet my life on, has come from people, my core family, my core community of well-intentioned adults. It has come from their beliefs that were handed down from their family. There's a lineage of beliefs we buy into that aren't fact-checked. Do we still believe what we've been told and conditioned to believe? Do these beliefs still hold up to the current world environment? We rarely reexamine the beliefs that govern our lives, govern our hearts, inform how we parent, inform how we love. How much of what I know is fact, sage advice, or information that will actually help me win the game of life, and how much of it is authentic to who I really am? How much of it reflects my essence, my deepest JOY?

You're Welcome

I'm sitting in the bathtub. Working to grow, feeling the things that I need to heal. To release them, extracting the lesson. Very proud of the work I put in to feel more delicious, more alive, more a Technicolor neon expression of the full multitude of every expanse of the rainbow. Starting with the ownership that there are multiple yet equanimous eyes in the me that I am learning and working diligently to, and allowing to touch softly, ME. So instead of control-freaking the day, which was a giant gold star for one of the now-smaller versions of myself that's still inside my heart but no longer is allowed to rule. I wake up with the sun, and I heed its sublime invitation to join her in the water.

I feel all the parts of this illumination dancing around my face. Plunging deep into my pores to connect. Organs, all the back-office services, all the ones who work diligently without my thought to keep the whole empire flowing. But not really shiny enough and obvious enough yet in our day-to-day lives to give window offices to. So, I allow the rays to come through my number one, my general, my first organ—my skin. It glides in. It illuminates every pore, every artery, every cell, every atom. My whole nervous system starts to relax. Gratitude flushes and flows in it. It bathes me with its visceral love.

I hear the birds chirping. They're serenading me, reminding me that we're all alive. I smile from ear to ear, waking up everyone else, letting them know it's time to go to work. It's another day. The army inside me, the team around me, the ancestors showing the path with every illuminated step. My angel family, like the little, tiny flying animals in all the Disney movies, are pulling the other dimensions of my many lives by the metaphorical shoulders and gliding me around as I feel more full of JOY.

"Good morning, Heart."

Rays of light, emerald beauty shining throughout, into all that energetically connect to her. I am now a glaze, a neon embodiment of all the wheels turning. Of my gut leading the way, inspiring me, lighting up my inner GPS. My feet feeling light. I'm flying with trust and faith that every step is guiding me closer and closer and deeper and deeper and more deliciously to my path, my mission. What I was deployed to do this go-round on earth school. It feels so good to feel so clear about so many of these details, and yet so alive with all that I don't know. As that is my love language, learning and growing, following the adventure that is life. That is the mission. That is the unraveling of the truth in every moment of its lower-than-expected peaks and its higher-than-remembered in faith and trust valleys. **RED**.

Those rays of light dance around my feet with gratitude. "You're welcome." I smile at them as I turn, feeling grateful that I had the ability to continue to nourish and love them as they nourish and love me. I remember to breathe, right? Sometimes I get excited and I forget, or let all the breath ferry and dance around in my chest. My back opening and expanding. The masculine side of me, feeling the need to take over. The mama creation energy: "No. Delegate. Ask for support." Right. I open up fully, as if I'm about to sing a song, and let the air move all the way down and through, and fall and turning on the excitement of the red everywhere. Connecting to the earth beneath my feet, and reminding me that I'm in my grounding, I am held. I grow with the roots that come up through me of every ancestor and all the lineage from every angle, every side, and every dimension. And every possible concept that we know thus far. Whew, ORANGE.

It fills me. I breathe through it. I'm alive, smiling at and reminding myself to abandon all the shame and the guilt, and the past information that was carried through for whatever intention at the time of survival. No longer needed in my full permission to be all the things, the full cornucopia of desires. Because I live in integrity, and what's great for me is great for all. As that's my wish. YELLOW. Sometimes a challenge. I am reminded that whenever I go there, to not try to be the best student and illuminate it through my thoughts, but to let it blossom from the seeds deep inside, the wisdom, the CLAIRGNOSIS that we have as we lean into our ancestral beings and all the lessons in every Akashic record. And we let it just germinate, then find roots. And then visualize these beautiful, tiny, tiny, almost-too-faint-to-see sunflowers growing and taking space, and pushing the ribs open and our chest forward.

Our back's leaning in to support this to the heavens. Sunflowers are growing, like the beanstalk, with every opportunity, and taking all the pleasure in reaching for the sun, and making a beautiful opening for our heart to fill our being with emeralds. Not the weight, but the rocks. With the beauty and the light, and the sound that we know in our hearts, the beating. That is source. That is our beloved. As it was said, at first there was a sound. And the word, and the word was Spirit. Our heartbeat, and the emerald light that connects to all of Earth and all of nature.

We visualize ourselves walking through nature, forest bathing. Letting our eyes lovingly take in all of the GREEN. Feeling our heartbeat, like a drum that guides our steps, and the perfect pace with the trust and the faith that our inner GPS is guiding us to win the game of life. Which is to learn to be

IT, that everything IS everything. That we are all aligned, that everything, every moment, every second, is our teacher. From that realization, I feel the heat from number one start to arise and turn with the snakes, coiling and tickling every part of myself to relax in its knowing. I connect deeper and deeper as I expand fully. And then everything that releases in me, every tear, sweat, excitement, every orifice is open. Everything is alive with what can be, what has been, and how all of that comes together in the spirit of the song of our hearts.

We're leaning all the way back, and we're breathing so fully, and everything is rising. All the colors now blending to this gorgeous connection to the BLUE color of the sea, and the sky everywhere. When the light opens up, it is JOY. Ah, alive. What else could we even need? Right? Because it's all right there. We have it all inside us, every jewel and every gem. Alive in us is all the light and sound, a full cacophony, right? A symphony of the imperfect perfection of the connection to us. Blending completely in every dimension, and in every sphere that we are nature.

We bring that lapis energy, and it sings through our hearts. And it connects to the sky. We are the sky, and we are the ocean. Connecting to every spirit that rules all of nature. That's alive in our DNA connection to that beautiful ancestral ring that dances in all of us, and that guides us.

And then the vibrations and tones and harmonics of those sounds create a brighter light in the sky and invites the clouds to release, and thus connect to the things in our body that need releasing. The tears, the secretions, the sweat, the past. And all its glory now gets to ring out and leave us the jewel of the lessons, and the supplements for our internal selves. And the knowing inside our hearts. And then it gets to be released with all the other files of something that we can lean into now to teach. To guide, starting with reminders to ourselves. That now that we've reached this higher place, through singing, through ascending, through the sky, through the clouds and all the things holding us in all the realms. As above, so below. And now the invitation and everything is racing, slithering higher, circling, dancing, spiraling.

Even through our voices . Even through the hearing and the listening, which is intimacy, we go higher. We're now reaching our regal selves, our royalty, our connection. We feel our parasympathetic nervous system chill. We feel the fight-or-flight we carry around like the harsh drum in our hearts. Like the harsh drum in our hearts beating to round up the tribes and tell all the other areas to be still. To not move. To not make a sound. We're fighting from survival. To now releasing to the belief that what we heal in one direction, we heal in seven, in each way, ancestral to whatever's birthing from us in our creations. Now we sit in a lighter perspective, carrying so much less with us. There's not as much room in the higher realms. You can't bring as much with you, because there's so much there for us to pull into our now-selves. The ME, the I AM, that's building to a giant me that connects passionately, curiously to the truth of who we really, really, really are. To what we were named the first time our soul was formed. To create would bring up, bring out, bring forth new change, new opportunities, new growth.

Now we sit in our third eye. We're nestled in the hammock of the lower realms of that experience. We look through the eye of the out, and the eye that goes in. We feel and we see with JOY, gratitude, and no judgment for what we've learned thus far. We sit in these times that we are given to work with, when things feel complicated and murky, to go in deeper. To sit in the bathtub, meditating on the rainbow, and the rest of it all just opening up to the world. **INDIGO**.

Just connect to the knowing. The deep, deep, deep below the ocean. Below the earth, that we can feel with our feet. And we sit in that relaxation, in that rest, in that trust, in that faith. In that truth of Grace, the embodiment of Grace. The just feeling grateful that there's nothing else to do right now but be still. To pray as an outward message of need and gratitude to Spirit. Sitting in the contemplation of the soft and quiet, listening to our Love speaking back to us.

And as we really rest without any thoughts that are triggering a reaction from their stimulus, we glide deeper into the seventh place, the place where we're carried and we're nestled. We are inside the rainbow, inside the inclusions of a rainbow revealing quartz, being suspended by things we can't even feel below us or around us. Nestled in the womblike space of creation, of every opportunity. Of every bit of knowledge with everything. And we go into a transcendental state of rest; we're without any movement that's obvious to the needs of our waking self. We are receiving on a level greater than we can even fathom.

ULTRAVIOLET.

You breathe it all in, in a beautiful circle, and whichever number feels resonant to you,

1

2

3

4

5

6

7

we pause as it gathers below our feet. We pull it up and hold it in a ball of red light. As we feel it, start at the base. And tickle and dance and breathe, all the way up through our crown, to a pause for whatever feels right. And then back down the front body and breathe. And circling this delicious oval of breath, and pause as you need it, until you feel restored to factory settings. I say to me,

"You're welcome."

TOOL

Transforming PATTERNS

These exercises can be performed at any point in time but are especially potent at the beginning of a new year, new life phase, new moon, or just when you're feeling like you need a tune-up.

REFLECT

Reflect on your pattern of behaviors over the past few months and write down those that you want to leave behind. Don't judge them. They aren't "negative," and you don't need to beat yourself up more than you already have. But they are things you don't want in your life anymore. Make a list of the patterns that are no longer serving you, that you are leaving in the past. Once finished, take a moment to read your list—then put it to the side.

RENEW

Write down moments from the past few months (especially the difficult ones) that were hard lessons learned, but lessons valuable enough to carry into the months ahead. What happened? What did you learn? What are the pearls of wisdom, even from painful moments? These are the experiences of growth that you are most proud of and intend to bring with you into the new year. Make a list of all these lessons. Feel what it feels like to embody these qualities and their wisdom.

RISE

This third and final list is about declaring what you want to experience in the coming months. You want to see and feel this new life as if it is already happening. What is the brilliant, beautiful future going to bring? Write these statements down in the present tense:

I live life fully in JOY.

I'm having so much fun at the party celebrating my promotion!

Write in the present tense so that it's baked in. You are writing what is brewing and percolating. Not *I want to move into a two-bedroom home,* but *I live in a beautiful two-bedroom home, with tons of light for my plants.* Read what you've written without judgment. . . . Read with reflection. Close your eyes to see the story each item on the list represents—watch the scenes of your future play out. This is your life. This is what your future looks like. Feel every detail. What is the temperature, the smell in the air? How does your body feel? Let the smile settle on your face and breathe into this feeling. The future is becoming your present. Once all three lists are completed and contemplated, purify and sanctify them through fire. You are going to burn them, one at a time, feeling the release of all that is on the list, all that is leaving. Sealing in what you are carrying forward and embodying what is to be—what has blossomed within you.

Please burn your three lists in something safe. Throw them into an existing fire (fireplace, bonfire), or let them burn into a fire-safe (metal or concrete) container.

Before you reconnect with other people after this ritual, take some time to sit with yourself. Thank yourself and give yourself a hug. Be present in your body. As a final step, go to a mirror, look yourself in the eyes, and recommit to loving the shit out of yourself for another three hundred and sixty-five days.

"Grace, I got you."

When you feel ready to see other people, hug everyone around you, have fun, and radiate love. Smile, dance, find some stars to gaze at. And most importantly, laugh. The way you start this new period of your life sets the tone.

Start it JOYfully!

Xo_ox

DEDICATED

Michelle Karshan

Warren Bruce Harry

Caitlin Karshan

Riva Nyri Précil

Mikala Leaf McLean

Raiden Wolf McLean

Georgia Petit Miguel

Usher Raymond V

Naviyd Ely Raymond

Jasmine Giordani

Khalib Holt

Jaylen Holt

Loa Oraia Alexis

Afoudayi Bila Alexi

TJS's STARTING FIVE

And just like all the creatives, framily that it was my pleasure to support through their processes, I needed a ton of encouraging support and sometimes a stern . . . *You got this.* The ones who were there for countless hours of reassurance that I could do this and reminders of why I wanted to in the first place, so I did not give up. Some of you literally held me up when I needed to be held up and then metaphorically held my hair back when I was leaning over the toilet. LOL.

Ahmir Thompson

Aiyisha Obafemi

Alec Kugler, for the cover photo.

Anita Kopacz

Brooke Amber Johnson

Deirdre Campbell

Jaha Johnson

Jaspre Guest—thank you for seeing ME and IT from the very beginning.

Jayson Jackson

Jimmy Soni

Julia Kadarusman-Khan

Kelvin "Pos" Mercer

La Shell Wooten

Lauren Rodman

Manish Vora

Marnie Nir

Meg Thompson—thank you, thank you and again . . . Thank you.

Rae Richman

Raiden Wolf McLean: Thank you for creating my happy Toolbox.

Suzanne Potts

Tracey Williams

Yo, B! Thank you for bringing my HEART, BRAIN, and EGO to life.

THE ANDSCAPE TEAM

Aliya S. King	Tonya Agurto
Jennifer Levesque	Olivia Zavitson
Raina Kelley	Amy King

THANK YOU

Andy Youmans	Kae Burke
Annie Kolatkar	Kamaal Fareed
Ant Demby	Loren Chodosh
Beija Velez	Ludwig Miguel
Bita Khorrami	Lysa Cooper
Bob Roth	Martha Snyder
Bryan "Charlie Brown" Higgins	Mege Posner
Carissa Schumacher	Mera Chooniedass
Caron Veazey	Michael Hebb
Chaka Zulu	Michael Nourse
Charlotte James	Michelle Rivers
Chris Rock	Miki Agrawal
Ciarra Pardo	Moj Mahdara
Delphine Fawundu	Monique Nelson
Dr. Josh Kantor	Natalie Bello
Dr. Maya Angelou	Nicole Fuller
Edosa Raymond Onaghise	Nona Aquan
Galaxia Barraza	Oasa Duverney
Iris Smith	Olivia Fischa
Jac Benson	Patrice Lighter
Jadah Carroll	Patti Penn
Jana Roemer	Ramesh Tarun
Janene Outlaw	Reika Alexander
Jeffrey Zurofsky	Rene McLean
Jo Anderson	Rodrigo Corral
Joe Wong	Rosaliz Jimenez

Roya Rastegar

Ruth Heinz

Samantha Rose Stein

Sari Teitelbaum Jackson

Satya Twena

Siedeh St. Foxie

Shawn "HOV" Carter

Sheena Lester

Threnur Holman

Tina Farris

Usher Raymond IV

Yvonna Kopacz-Wright